CONTENTS

The Habit Blueprint: Small Changes, Big Results	1
Introduction: The Power of Habits	3
Chapter 1: The Science of Habit Formation	10
Chapter 2: Identifying Your Keystone Habits	26
Chapter 3: Crafting Your Habit Blueprint	43
Chapter 4: The Power of Small Wins	60
Chapter 5: Overcoming Resistance: Breaking Bad Habits	77
Chapter 6: Building Resilience: Sticking to Your New Habits	95
Chapter 7: Habits in Health and Wellness	113
Chapter 8: Habits for Productivity and Time Management	128
Chapter 9: Social Habits: Building Strong Relationships	143
Chapter 10: The Long Game: Turning Habits into a Lifestyle	159
Conclusion: The Future You Through Habits	173
Appendix:	180
Final Thoughts	187

THE HABIT BLUEPRINT: SMALL CHANGES, BIG RESULTS

Master the Art of Daily Routines to Transform Your Life

By: David Avera

About the Author

David Avera is a dedicated Fire Captain and a proud United States Air Force veteran. Throughout his military career, David understood the importance of forming good habits, a practice that became integral to his success. Now, in his leadership role within the fire service, he continues to rely on these habits to maintain a critical edge when lives are on the line. David's commitment to discipline, teamwork, and excellence has been the cornerstone of his career, both in the military and in his service as a firefighter.

Writing books has always been a passion for David, and through his work, he aims to share the knowledge he has gained, helping others achieve the same success with which he has been blessed.

INTRODUCTION: THE POWER OF HABITS

Habits are the automatic actions we take every day, often without thinking, that shape our behaviors and outcomes over time. They are routines or practices that we repeatedly perform until they become ingrained in our daily lives. Habits can be positive, like exercising regularly, or negative, like procrastination. Whether we realize it or not, habits play a significant role in determining our overall success and well-being.

At their core, habits are formed through a process called the "habit loop," which involves three stages: the cue, the routine, and the reward. The **cue** is the trigger that initiates the habit, the **routine** is the behavior that follows, and the **reward** is the benefit you gain from completing the habit. For example, if your morning alarm goes off (cue), you might immediately head to the kitchen for coffee (routine), and the satisfaction of that first sip provides the reward. Over time, this loop becomes automatic, making coffee part of your daily ritual.

Habits are **critical for success** because they determine the small, consistent actions that accumulate into significant outcomes. In any area of life—whether it's health, career, relationships, or personal growth—habits create the foundation for progress. Here's why habits are so essential:

1. **Consistency Beats Motivation**: Success is not about one-off moments of brilliance; it's about showing up consistently. Habits allow you to perform actions regularly without relying on fleeting motivation or willpower. Once a habit is established, you don't have to think or convince yourself to do something—you

just do it. This consistency is the backbone of progress in any endeavor.
2. **Small Changes, Big Impact**: The power of habits lies in their compounding effect. Small, seemingly insignificant actions can add up over time to produce substantial results. For example, reading just 10 pages of a book every day may not seem like much, but over a year, that's 3,650 pages—or the equivalent of 10 to 12 books. Whether it's saving a bit of money daily or doing a short workout, these tiny habits accumulate into massive change over time.
3. **Habits Shape Identity**: Our habits define who we are. If you regularly work out, you identify as someone who is fit and healthy. If you consistently meet deadlines and plan your work, you identify as someone who is organized and productive. By building positive habits, you can begin to shape the identity of the person you want to become, which in turn reinforces the behavior.
4. **Habits Create Freedom**: While habits may seem restrictive at first, they actually provide freedom by reducing decision fatigue. When a behavior becomes a habit, it frees up mental energy that would otherwise be spent making decisions. This efficiency allows you to focus on more important tasks, fostering creativity, productivity, and even relaxation.

In summary, habits are the building blocks of success. They allow us to achieve consistency, harness the power of compounding actions, shape our identities, and free up mental space for more meaningful pursuits. By consciously building and refining our habits, we can create the foundation for long-term success in every aspect of life.

How Small Changes Can Have a Significant Impact Over Time (The Compounding Effect)

The concept of the **compounding effect** refers to the way

small, incremental actions or improvements accumulate over time to produce significant, often transformational, results. This principle is most commonly associated with finance, where interest earned on an investment grows exponentially as it accumulates. However, the compounding effect applies to virtually every area of life, from health and fitness to productivity and personal growth. By making small, consistent changes, you can achieve monumental shifts in your life over time.

The Power of Small Improvements

One of the most compelling examples of the compounding effect is the idea of getting just 1% better every day. While a 1% improvement may seem trivial or inconsequential in the short term, its long-term impact can be staggering. Mathematically, if you improve by 1% each day, you will be 37 times better by the end of the year. This principle highlights how small changes, when applied consistently, can lead to exponential growth.

Let's take health and fitness as an example. Imagine you start by doing five minutes of exercise a day. At first, this might seem insignificant—how can five minutes make a difference? But if you gradually increase your exercise time by just one minute each day, you would be exercising for over an hour within two months. Over the course of a year, this habit could completely transform your health, leading to increased strength, better cardiovascular health, and improved mental well-being.

Habits and the Compound Effect

Habits are the vehicles that drive the compounding effect in our lives. When we build small, positive habits, they begin to accumulate and grow, often without us even realizing it. The compounding effect works both ways, though—it can either work for you or against you. Positive habits, like saving a small portion of your income regularly or reading a few pages of a book each night, can lead to substantial gains over time. On the flip side, negative habits, like indulging in unhealthy snacks or procrastinating for just 10 minutes each day, can gradually erode progress and lead to significant setbacks.

This idea is often referred to as the "snowball effect." Just as a snowball rolling down a hill gathers more snow and increases in size, so too do our habits and actions accumulate momentum over time. A small habit, when repeated consistently, gains power and influence, impacting various areas of your life. For example, the simple habit of going to bed 30 minutes earlier could lead to better sleep quality, improved mood, and increased productivity, which in turn could enhance your career and relationships.

The Ripple Effect

Small changes also create ripple effects, influencing not just the area in which the change occurs but other parts of your life as well. For instance, adopting a habit of daily gratitude journaling might initially seem small, but over time it can shift your mindset to one of positivity and contentment. This positive shift can improve your relationships, reduce stress, and even enhance your physical health as you begin to perceive life more optimistically.

The ripple effect of small changes can also inspire those around you. Your commitment to self-improvement, even through small steps, can motivate friends, family, and colleagues to make changes in their own lives, further amplifying the impact of your actions.

In conclusion, small changes are not to be underestimated. The compounding effect shows that even the tiniest of improvements, when repeated consistently over time, can result in dramatic and lasting transformations. Whether it's improving your health, finances, career, or personal relationships, the key is consistency and patience. By focusing on incremental progress rather than overnight success, you harness the power of the compounding effect, allowing small changes to build into significant, life-altering results.

Introducing the Habit Blueprint

Imagine you want to build a house. You wouldn't just start laying bricks randomly or assembling walls haphazardly—you'd start with a blueprint. A blueprint is a carefully designed plan that guides the construction process, ensuring that everything is built on a strong foundation and works together harmoniously. Now, think of your life goals and aspirations in the same way. To achieve them, you need more than just good intentions—you need a clear, actionable plan. This is where the **Habit Blueprint** comes into play.

The **Habit Blueprint** is a strategic framework for building lasting habits that align with your goals and lead to long-term success. Just like a construction blueprint, it provides the structure, direction, and tools you need to transform small, daily actions into significant life changes. It is a step-by-step guide that helps you design, implement, and maintain habits that are not only sustainable but also deeply connected to the outcomes you desire.

The Habit Blueprint is built on the premise that success isn't achieved through one grand, sweeping action but rather through the consistent application of small, deliberate habits over time. By following the blueprint, you'll learn how to create habits that are custom-tailored to your needs, designed to be easily integrated into your life, and scalable as your goals evolve.

Key Elements of the Habit Blueprint

1. **Clarity of Purpose**: The first step in the Habit Blueprint is identifying your "why." Before you can

build effective habits, you need a clear understanding of what you want to achieve and why it matters to you. Whether your goal is to improve your health, advance in your career, or strengthen your relationships, the Habit Blueprint helps you define your purpose so that your habits have a clear direction.

2. **Start Small, Think Big**: One of the fundamental principles of the Habit Blueprint is to start with small, manageable habits. These micro-habits, such as reading for five minutes a day or taking a short walk, may seem minor, but they lay the foundation for bigger changes. The blueprint emphasizes the power of incremental progress—small habits, when repeated consistently, compound over time to create significant results.

3. **Designing the Habit Loop**: The Habit Blueprint teaches you how to create an effective habit loop, which consists of three core components: the **cue**, the **routine**, and the **reward**. This loop is the engine that drives habit formation. The blueprint helps you identify cues that trigger your habits, establish routines that are easy to follow, and set up rewards that reinforce positive behavior, making the habit stick.

4. **Habit Stacking**: One of the most powerful strategies in the Habit Blueprint is habit stacking, which involves linking a new habit to an existing one. For example, if you already brush your teeth every morning (an established habit), you might stack a new habit like practicing gratitude right after. By attaching new habits to established routines, you make them easier to adopt and integrate into your daily life.

5. **Accountability and Adjustment**: The Habit Blueprint isn't static—it's a living document that evolves with you. As you progress, the blueprint encourages you to reflect on your habits, track your results, and

make adjustments as necessary. This continuous feedback loop ensures that your habits remain aligned with your goals and that you can pivot when life circumstances change.
6. **Long-Term Vision**: The ultimate goal of the Habit Blueprint is to turn habits into a lifestyle. It's not just about short-term gains; it's about creating sustainable routines that support your long-term vision. By focusing on habits that align with your core values and aspirations, the blueprint helps you design a life that reflects who you truly want to be.

The Habit Blueprint is your personalized roadmap to success. It breaks down the overwhelming process of habit change into simple, actionable steps that lead to lasting transformation. Throughout this book, we'll dive deeper into each component of the blueprint, giving you the tools and strategies you need to take control of your habits, achieve your goals, and build the life you envision—one small, powerful step at a time.

CHAPTER 1: THE SCIENCE OF HABIT FORMATION

How Habits Are Formed: Understanding Triggers, Routines, and Rewards

Habits are the invisible architecture of our daily lives. They shape our actions, decisions, and, ultimately, our outcomes. But how exactly are habits formed? The process of habit formation can be understood through a simple but powerful model known as the **habit loop**, which consists of three main components: triggers, routines, and rewards. By understanding how these elements interact, we can learn to build positive habits, break negative ones, and design our lives more intentionally.

The Habit Loop: An Overview

The habit loop is a neurological pattern that governs every habit. This loop consists of:

1. **Trigger (Cue)**: The trigger is the event that initiates the habit. It can be a specific time of day, an emotional state, an external environment, or any other signal that prompts the behavior.
2. **Routine (Behavior)**: The routine is the actual behavior or action that follows the trigger. This is the habit itself —what you do in response to the trigger.
3. **Reward**: The reward is the benefit you gain from performing the habit. It's what makes the behavior worthwhile, providing satisfaction or relief that reinforces the habit loop.

Understanding this loop is crucial because it reveals the underlying mechanics of habit formation and helps us manipulate the process to create or change habits.

Triggers: The Starting Point of Habits

Triggers, also known as cues, are the starting point of every habit. They are the signals that tell your brain to go into automatic mode and initiate a particular habit. Triggers can be categorized into several types:

1. **Time-Based Triggers**: These are triggers that occur at a specific time of day. For example, brushing your teeth every morning after waking up is typically triggered by the time of day (morning).
2. **Location-Based Triggers**: These triggers are related to your environment or surroundings. For example, entering your kitchen might trigger the habit of grabbing a snack, or sitting at your desk might trigger the habit of checking your email.
3. **Emotional Triggers**: Emotions often serve as powerful triggers for habits. For instance, feeling stressed might trigger the habit of eating comfort food, while feeling bored might trigger the habit of scrolling through social media.
4. **Social Triggers**: The people around us can also act as triggers. For example, seeing a friend order a dessert might trigger you to do the same, or hearing your colleagues talk about their weekend plans might trigger the habit of making your own plans.
5. **Preceding Event Triggers**: These triggers are actions or events that directly precede the habit. For example, finishing dinner might trigger the habit of watching TV, or completing a workout might trigger the habit of drinking a protein shake.

Triggers are powerful because they put the brain into a state of readiness, signaling that it's time to execute a specific routine. Identifying the triggers associated with your habits is the first step in understanding how those habits form and persist.

Routines: The Behavior That Follows

The routine is the actual behavior that you perform in response to the trigger. This is the most visible part of the habit loop—the action that people typically refer to as the "habit." Routines can be incredibly varied, ranging from simple actions like brushing your teeth to more complex behaviors like following a workout regimen or writing daily journal entries.

Routines can be classified into two broad categories:

1. **Positive Routines**: These are behaviors that contribute positively to your life, such as exercising, reading, or practicing mindfulness. These routines align with your goals and values, helping you move closer to the person you want to become.
2. **Negative Routines**: These are behaviors that have a detrimental effect, such as smoking, overeating, or procrastinating. These routines often lead to outcomes that are contrary to your goals and can hinder your progress.

The routine is the most critical part of the habit loop because it is the behavior that needs to be established, maintained, or changed. However, the routine alone doesn't create a habit; it must be consistently triggered and rewarded to become ingrained.

Rewards: The Reinforcing Mechanism

Rewards are the third and final component of the habit loop. The reward is what makes the habit loop worth repeating. It provides satisfaction, relief, or pleasure, reinforcing the behavior and making it more likely that you will perform the routine again in the future.

Rewards can be immediate or delayed, intrinsic or extrinsic:

1. **Immediate Rewards**: These are rewards that occur

right after the routine is completed. For example, the feeling of relaxation after a workout or the taste of a sweet treat after dinner.
2. **Delayed Rewards**: These rewards are not immediately apparent but accumulate over time. For instance, the long-term health benefits of regular exercise or the financial security that comes from saving money.
3. **Intrinsic Rewards**: These are internal rewards, such as feelings of pride, satisfaction, or fulfillment. Intrinsic rewards are often the most sustainable because they are tied to your inner values and sense of self.
4. **Extrinsic Rewards**: These are external rewards, such as praise, recognition, or tangible rewards like money or gifts. While extrinsic rewards can be motivating, they may not be as enduring as intrinsic rewards.

The reward is crucial because it tells your brain that the routine is worth remembering. Over time, your brain begins to associate the trigger with the reward, making the routine more automatic. If the reward is satisfying enough, the habit loop is reinforced, and the behavior becomes ingrained.

The Habit Loop in Action

Let's consider a common habit to illustrate the habit loop in action: checking your phone for notifications.

Trigger: You feel a slight buzz in your pocket (a notification).
Routine: You take out your phone and check the notification.
Reward: You get a dopamine hit from reading a new message, seeing a like on social media, or receiving an interesting update.

This loop might seem harmless, but over time, it can become a deeply ingrained habit, leading you to check your phone constantly, even when no notifications are present. The key to breaking or modifying such a habit lies in understanding and altering one or more components of the loop.

Manipulating the Habit Loop

By understanding the habit loop, you can start to take control of your habits—either by creating new ones, changing existing ones, or breaking bad ones.

1. **Changing the Trigger**: If you want to change a habit, start by altering the trigger. For instance, if you want to reduce the habit of snacking when stressed, identify the situations that trigger stress and find alternative ways to cope, such as taking a walk or practicing deep breathing.
2. **Modifying the Routine**: If the routine is the problem, look for ways to change the behavior. For example, if you habitually check your phone first thing in the morning, you might try substituting this routine with a more positive behavior, such as reading or meditating.
3. **Adjusting the Reward**: Sometimes, the reward isn't satisfying enough to reinforce the habit. In this case, you can modify the reward to make it more compelling. For example, if you're trying to establish a habit of exercising, reward yourself with something enjoyable after each workout, such as a healthy smoothie or a relaxing bath.

Habits are formed through a cycle of triggers, routines, and rewards—a process that is both simple and complex. Simple in that it involves just three steps, yet complex in how deeply these steps can become embedded in our daily lives. By understanding this habit loop, you can begin to take control of your behaviors, design new habits that support your goals, and break free from those that hold you back. Whether you're looking to build a habit of daily exercise, improve your productivity, or quit a bad habit, mastering the habit loop is the first step toward lasting change.

The Neurological Basis of Habits: Understanding the Habit Loop

Habits are deeply embedded in our brains, shaping much of our daily behavior, often without conscious thought. The process by which habits are formed is known as the **habit loop**, a neurological cycle that includes three main components: the **cue (or trigger)**, the **routine (or behavior)**, and the **reward**. This loop is fundamental to how our brains automate repetitive actions, freeing up mental energy for other tasks. By understanding the neurological basis of habits, we can gain insight into why habits are so powerful and how we can create or change them to improve our lives.

The Brain and Habits: The Role of the Basal Ganglia

The habit loop is rooted in the brain's **basal ganglia**, a group of structures located deep within the cerebral hemispheres. The basal ganglia play a key role in motor control, learning, and habit formation. Research has shown that once a behavior becomes a habit, the basal ganglia take over the responsibility of executing that behavior, allowing the rest of the brain to focus on other tasks.

This automation is crucial because it conserves cognitive energy. Imagine if you had to consciously think about every single step involved in brushing your teeth each morning or driving to work—you'd be mentally exhausted by the end of the day. Instead, once a behavior becomes habitual, the brain essentially "outsources" it to the basal ganglia, allowing you to perform the task automatically while thinking about other things.

However, this automation also makes habits resistant to change. Because the brain prefers efficiency, it will continue to rely on these deeply ingrained habits unless a conscious effort is made to alter the habit loop.

The Habit Loop: Cue, Routine, and Reward

1. Cue (Trigger): The Starting Point of the Habit Loop

The **cue** is the first component of the habit loop and serves as the trigger that initiates the behavior. It could be anything—an external event, an emotional state, or even a specific time of day. For example, hearing your alarm clock in the morning may trigger the habit of getting out of bed, or feeling stressed might trigger the habit of reaching for a snack.

Neurologically, cues activate specific regions of the brain that prepare the body and mind to execute the habitual routine. Once the cue is detected, the brain shifts into a mode where it expects a particular behavior to follow. This expectation is why cues are so powerful in driving habits. For instance, when you hear the sound of your phone buzzing, your brain immediately expects the behavior of checking your notifications, and you often do so without conscious thought.

Understanding the importance of cues is vital for both creating and changing habits. If you want to establish a new habit, you can intentionally design cues that trigger the desired behavior. Conversely, if you're trying to break a bad habit, identifying and disrupting the cue is the first step toward change.

2. Routine (Behavior): The Action That Becomes a Habit

The **routine** is the behavior itself—the action you take in response to the cue. This is the most visible part of the habit loop and the part that people usually refer to when they talk about habits. Routines can range from simple actions, such as brushing your teeth or checking your email, to more complex behaviors, like going for a run or completing a work project.

Once a habit is formed, the routine becomes automatic, meaning it requires little to no conscious effort to execute. This is where the basal ganglia come into play, as they take over the execution of the routine. This automation is what allows habits to persist even when you're not actively thinking about them. The key to changing a habit lies in altering the routine while keeping the same cue and reward. For example, if stress triggers you to eat unhealthy snacks, you can try replacing the routine of snacking with a healthier behavior, like taking a walk or practicing deep breathing. The cue (stress) and reward (relief) remain the same, but the routine changes.

3. **Reward: The Reinforcing Component of the Habit Loop**

The **reward** is the final and most critical part of the habit loop. It provides the positive reinforcement that makes the brain want to repeat the behavior in the future. Rewards can be physical (such as the taste of food), emotional (such as a sense of accomplishment), or psychological (such as relief from stress).

Neurologically, rewards trigger the release of **dopamine**, a neurotransmitter associated with pleasure and reinforcement. When your brain receives a reward, it strengthens the neural connections associated with the routine, making it more likely that you will repeat the behavior the next time the cue appears. This is why habits become so deeply ingrained over time—each repetition of the habit loop reinforces the behavior at a neurological level.

However, the reward must be satisfying enough for the brain to remember and repeat the habit. If the reward isn't compelling, the brain is less likely to store the routine as a habit. This is why habits that offer immediate rewards (like the satisfaction of eating junk food) can be hard to break, while habits with delayed rewards (like exercising) can be more challenging to form initially.

How Understanding the Neurological Basis of Habits Helps You Create or Change Them

Understanding the habit loop at a neurological level gives you the tools to both create new habits and change existing ones. Here's how this knowledge can be applied:

1. Creating New Habits

To create a new habit, you need to establish a strong habit loop: a clear cue, a defined routine, and a satisfying reward.

Step 1: Choose a Cue: Start by selecting a consistent cue that will trigger the behavior. It should be something that naturally occurs in your day, like a specific time, location, or emotional state. For example, if you want to start meditating, you could choose to do it right after waking up (time-based cue) or after brushing your teeth (preceding event cue).

Step 2: Design the Routine: Make sure the routine is simple and easy to execute, especially in the beginning. The simpler the behavior, the easier it is for the brain to automate it. For example, if you're trying to establish a habit of exercising, start with just 10 minutes a day.

Step 3: Establish a Reward: The reward is crucial for reinforcing the habit. Choose something that you will genuinely look forward to. If the behavior itself doesn't provide an immediate reward (e.g., exercise), create an artificial reward that motivates you, like enjoying a smoothie or a relaxing shower afterward.

2. Changing Existing Habits

To change an existing habit, you need to identify the elements of the habit loop and tweak them strategically.

Step 1: Identify the Cue: Start by identifying what triggers the habit. Is it stress, boredom, a particular time of day, or something else? Understanding the cue will help you disrupt the loop.

Step 2: Change the Routine: Once you've identified the cue, focus on changing the routine while keeping the same cue and reward. For example, if you tend to watch TV after work to relax, try substituting that routine with a healthier alternative, like reading or going for a walk.

Step 3: Keep the Reward: Make sure the new routine provides a similar reward to the one you're replacing. If the reward is emotional (such as relaxation), ensure the new behavior offers a comparable feeling of relief or satisfaction.

3. **Breaking Bad Habits**

Breaking a bad habit requires interrupting the habit loop, particularly by targeting the cue and reward.

Step 1: Remove or Alter the Cue: Try to eliminate the cue from your environment or replace it with something less triggering. For example, if seeing a snack jar in your kitchen triggers unhealthy eating, remove the jar or replace it with a bowl of fruit.

Step 2: Disrupt the Reward: If you can't remove the cue, focus on diminishing the reward. For example, if overeating is triggered by stress, find ways to make the reward less satisfying by reminding yourself of the negative consequences or creating alternative coping mechanisms.

Habits are deeply rooted in our brain's neurological pathways, governed by the habit loop of cue, routine, and reward. By understanding how this loop works and how it is reinforced in the brain, we can take control of our habits—whether by creating new, positive ones, changing existing routines, or breaking free from bad habits. The key is to identify the elements of the habit loop, make deliberate adjustments, and consistently reinforce these changes until they become second nature.

Examples of Powerful Habits That Have Changed Lives

Habits, whether small or large, have the potential to significantly shape our lives. Over time, these seemingly insignificant routines accumulate and lead to profound transformations. Some habits are so powerful that they have been instrumental in the success of prominent figures, improved the well-being of countless individuals, and even transformed societies. In this section, we will explore several examples of powerful habits that have changed lives, illustrating the impact that disciplined routines can have on personal growth, health, career, and relationships.

1. Morning Routines of Successful People

A powerful habit that has changed the lives of many successful people is the establishment of a structured morning routine. How one starts the day can set the tone for the rest of it, and many high achievers swear by their carefully crafted morning rituals.

For example, **Tim Ferriss**, entrepreneur and author of *The 4-Hour Workweek*, starts his day with a combination of mindfulness, exercise, and productivity-enhancing activities. His morning routine includes practices like meditation, journaling, and a short workout, which help him enter the day with a clear mind and energized body. Similarly, **Oprah Winfrey** practices a morning ritual that includes meditation, gratitude journaling, and exercise. These habits have helped both Ferriss and Winfrey build resilience, maintain mental clarity, and sustain high levels of productivity.

The key takeaway here is that starting the day with a routine designed to foster mental, emotional, and physical well-being can have a compounding positive effect on the rest of your day. Whether it's a quick morning workout, meditation, or just 10 minutes of planning, creating a consistent morning habit can transform your life by setting the foundation for success.

2. The Habit of Reading

The habit of daily reading has been life-changing for many individuals, particularly those in leadership positions. **Bill Gates**, the co-founder of Microsoft, is known for his voracious reading habit, reportedly reading 50 books a year. Gates credits reading with providing him with knowledge, inspiration, and new perspectives that have informed his decisions and shaped his worldview.

Similarly, **Warren Buffett**, one of the most successful investors in the world, has built a lifelong habit of reading extensively. He has famously said that he spends 80% of his day reading. Buffett believes that reading allows him to gain a competitive edge by staying informed and continuously learning.

Reading can help individuals expand their knowledge, stimulate creativity, and improve cognitive function. It has the power to transform minds, open new opportunities, and even inspire life-changing decisions. For those looking to grow intellectually or professionally, cultivating a daily reading habit can be a key driver of success.

3. Exercise as a Keystone Habit

Exercise is often referred to as a "keystone habit," meaning that it has the power to influence multiple areas of a person's life. Regular physical activity not only improves physical health but also enhances mental well-being, productivity, and emotional resilience. Countless people, from celebrities to everyday individuals, credit exercise as the foundation of their success and well-being.

Barack Obama, former President of the United States, is an example of someone who prioritized exercise even during the busiest times of his career. He reportedly worked out for 45 minutes each morning, alternating between strength training and cardio. This habit not only kept him physically fit but also helped him manage stress and maintain high energy levels throughout his demanding schedule.

Exercise boosts endorphins, which improves mood, reduces anxiety, and helps manage stress. Additionally, it enhances cognitive function by improving blood flow to the brain, which can lead to better decision-making and focus. For anyone looking to improve their physical and mental health, adopting a regular exercise routine can be transformative.

4. The Power of Gratitude

Gratitude is a simple but incredibly powerful habit that can shift perspectives and improve overall well-being. Studies have shown that practicing gratitude regularly can increase happiness, reduce depression, and strengthen relationships. It rewires the brain to focus on positive aspects of life, which in turn fosters a sense of contentment and fulfillment.

One example of someone who has harnessed the power of gratitude is **Tony Robbins**, a renowned motivational speaker and author. Robbins practices a morning ritual called "priming," which includes a period of gratitude where he reflects on three things he is grateful for each day. He believes that starting the day with gratitude helps set a positive tone and energizes him to face challenges with a sense of purpose.

Gratitude journaling—writing down a few things you are thankful for each day—has been shown to increase long-term well-being by as much as 10%, according to research. This simple habit shifts attention away from negativity and scarcity, helping individuals cultivate a more positive and resilient mindset.

5. Journaling for Self-Reflection

Journaling is another habit that has changed lives by promoting self-reflection, clarity, and personal growth. Writing down thoughts, goals, and experiences allows individuals to process their emotions, organize their thoughts, and track their progress over time.

One notable advocate of journaling is **Tim Ferriss**, who incorporates this habit into his morning routine. Ferriss practices a type of journaling called "morning pages," where he writes three pages of stream-of-consciousness thoughts every morning. This practice helps him clear his mind, identify patterns in his thinking, and develop new ideas.

Similarly, **Benjamin Franklin** was known for his daily habit of journaling, which he used as a tool for self-improvement. He would reflect on his goals, his actions, and the virtues he wanted to cultivate, using his journal as a means of accountability and self-assessment.

Journaling provides an opportunity for introspection and helps individuals gain insight into their thoughts and behaviors. Over time, this habit can lead to greater self-awareness, better decision-making, and more focused personal growth.

6. Mindfulness and Meditation

The practice of mindfulness and meditation has become increasingly popular in recent years, with many individuals crediting it with transforming their mental health and emotional well-being. Meditation helps reduce stress, improve focus, and promote a sense of calm and inner peace.

Ray Dalio, the founder of Bridgewater Associates, one of the largest hedge funds in the world, is a strong advocate of meditation. Dalio has practiced Transcendental Meditation for decades and believes it has been instrumental in his success. He credits meditation with helping him manage stress, make better decisions, and maintain emotional balance.

Mindfulness and meditation have also been embraced by other high achievers, such as **Arianna Huffington**, founder of *The Huffington Post*, and **Jack Dorsey**, CEO of Twitter and Square. These individuals use meditation as a tool to enhance clarity, creativity, and resilience in the face of challenges.

Meditation allows individuals to cultivate a greater sense of awareness and presence, which can lead to better emotional regulation and a more focused mind. This habit can be particularly life-changing for those who struggle with stress, anxiety, or overthinking.

7. Fasting and Nutrition

Fasting and mindful nutrition have become life-changing habits for many people seeking to improve their health and longevity. **Dr. Jason Fung**, a nephrologist and author, has popularized the use of intermittent fasting as a method for weight loss and metabolic health. His research has shown that fasting can help regulate insulin levels, reduce inflammation, and promote autophagy, a process where the body cleans out damaged cells.

Similarly, **Hugh Jackman**, the actor famous for his role as Wolverine, uses intermittent fasting to maintain his physical fitness. By limiting his eating window and focusing on nutrient-dense foods, Jackman has been able to sustain a high level of energy and physical conditioning.

Fasting and mindful eating habits can lead to significant improvements in physical health, from weight management to enhanced longevity. These habits encourage individuals to develop a healthier relationship with food and improve their overall well-being.

These examples illustrate the transformative power of habits in a wide range of areas, from personal growth and productivity to health and well-being. Whether it's a structured morning routine, the habit of daily reading, regular exercise, or mindfulness, the key is consistency and intentionality. These powerful habits have not only changed the lives of the individuals who practice them but have also inspired millions of others to adopt similar routines. By integrating such habits into your life, you can take control of your actions and outcomes, ultimately shaping the life you want to live.

CHAPTER 2: IDENTIFYING YOUR KEYSTONE HABITS

Defining Keystone Habits: The Habits That Positively Impact Other Areas of Your Life

In the realm of personal development, the concept of **keystone habits** stands out as a particularly powerful tool for creating positive, far-reaching changes in one's life. A **keystone habit** is a foundational habit that triggers a chain reaction, positively influencing other behaviors and habits across multiple areas of your life. These habits are not necessarily the most important or challenging ones, but they serve as catalysts for broader improvements in productivity, health, relationships, and overall well-being.

The term "keystone habit" was popularized by Charles Duhigg in his book *The Power of Habit*. Duhigg explains that keystone habits have the ability to create small wins, which, when compounded, lead to significant transformations. These habits initiate a process of positive reinforcement, where the benefits of one habit spread to other aspects of life, often in ways that are not immediately obvious.

What Are Keystone Habits?

Keystone habits are specific behaviors that, once established, can trigger a cascade of other positive habits. For example, regular exercise is often considered a keystone habit because it not only improves physical health but also enhances mental clarity, boosts mood, encourages better eating habits, and even improves sleep patterns. By focusing on developing a keystone habit, you can create a ripple effect that improves multiple areas of your life with relatively little effort.

Keystone habits are powerful because they work on multiple

levels: they influence behavior, thought patterns, and even identity. Once established, they can help individuals become more disciplined, focused, and self-aware, which in turn leads to further positive changes. These habits often serve as the foundation for larger, long-term goals and are essential for achieving sustained success.

Characteristics of Keystone Habits

Keystone habits share a few key characteristics that make them uniquely effective in sparking widespread change:

1. **They Create a Ripple Effect**: The primary characteristic of keystone habits is their ability to influence other behaviors. For example, someone who starts exercising regularly may find that they also begin to eat healthier, sleep better, and feel more energized throughout the day. These secondary benefits extend beyond the original habit, creating a domino effect of positive outcomes.
2. **They Are Small but Significant**: Keystone habits are often simple and manageable to implement, which makes them easier to stick to. They don't require radical changes to your routine, yet they yield disproportionate results. For instance, making your bed every morning is a small action, but it sets a tone of discipline and accomplishment for the rest of the day.
3. **They Foster Confidence and Motivation**: Keystone habits generate small wins, which build momentum and foster self-confidence. When you see progress in one area, you become more motivated to tackle other challenges. These small victories create a positive feedback loop that encourages the continuation of good habits.
4. **They Promote Identity Shifts**: Keystone habits often lead to shifts in identity, as they reinforce the idea that you are the kind of person who engages in positive

behaviors. For example, someone who commits to daily journaling may begin to see themselves as more reflective and intentional, which can lead to additional positive changes in behavior.

Examples of Keystone Habits

To better understand the power of keystone habits, let's explore a few examples that have been shown to trigger positive changes across multiple areas of life.

1. **Exercise**

Regular physical activity is one of the most well-known keystone habits. Exercise doesn't just improve physical fitness; it also has a profound impact on mental health, productivity, and overall well-being. Studies have shown that people who exercise regularly are more likely to eat healthier, sleep better, and manage stress more effectively. Additionally, exercise boosts cognitive function, making it easier to focus and stay productive throughout the day.

For example, **Barack Obama**, during his presidency, prioritized a daily workout as a non-negotiable part of his routine. This keystone habit helped him manage the immense stress of his job, maintain his physical health, and enhance his mental clarity and decision-making abilities.

2. **Meditation**

Meditation is another powerful keystone habit that can have far-reaching effects. By practicing mindfulness or meditation regularly, individuals can reduce stress, improve emotional regulation, and increase their ability to focus. These benefits extend beyond the meditation practice itself and influence other aspects of life, such as relationships, work performance, and overall happiness.

Many high-achieving individuals, such as **Ray Dalio**, founder of Bridgewater Associates, credit meditation with helping them stay grounded and make better decisions. The habit of meditating consistently can lead to a more centered and balanced approach to life, which in turn can improve emotional resilience, interpersonal interactions, and productivity.

3. Journaling

Journaling is a keystone habit that promotes self-reflection, clarity, and intentionality. By taking the time to write down thoughts, goals, and reflections, individuals can gain insight into their emotions, behaviors, and aspirations. Journaling encourages mindfulness and self-awareness, which can lead to better decision-making, improved emotional health, and enhanced personal growth.

For example, **Tim Ferriss**, author and entrepreneur, practices journaling as part of his morning routine. By reflecting on his goals and mindset, Ferriss has been able to maintain focus, track progress, and cultivate a sense of gratitude, which positively impacts his productivity and well-being throughout the day.

4. Sleep Hygiene

Establishing good sleep hygiene is another keystone habit that can dramatically improve quality of life. Sleep affects nearly every aspect of physical and mental health, including cognitive function, mood, energy levels, and immune function. By prioritizing sleep and creating a consistent bedtime routine, individuals can improve their overall well-being and set the stage for success in other areas of life.

For example, adopting a habit of going to bed at the same

time each night, avoiding screens before bed, and creating a relaxing bedtime ritual can lead to better sleep quality. In turn, improved sleep can enhance cognitive performance, emotional regulation, and physical health, making it easier to maintain other positive habits, such as exercise and healthy eating.

5. **Daily Planning**

The habit of daily planning can also serve as a keystone habit. By taking just a few minutes each day to plan your tasks and priorities, you can gain a clearer sense of direction and reduce feelings of overwhelm. Daily planning helps individuals stay organized, focused, and productive, which can lead to better time management and achievement of long-term goals.

For instance, **Benjamin Franklin** was known for his habit of meticulously planning his day. He would begin each day by asking himself, "What good shall I do today?" This practice helped him stay focused on his goals and maintain a sense of purpose, ultimately contributing to his success as a statesman, inventor, and writer.

6. **Healthy Eating**

Developing a habit of healthy eating can have a domino effect on other areas of life, from physical health to mental clarity. When individuals prioritize nutritious foods, they often experience increased energy, improved mood, and better overall health. These benefits can lead to enhanced productivity, better sleep, and greater emotional resilience.

For example, individuals who commit to eating a balanced breakfast every morning often report feeling more energized and focused throughout the day. This simple habit can influence other behaviors, such as making healthier food choices at lunch and dinner and staying physically active.

How to Identify and Develop Keystone Habits

To identify and develop keystone habits in your own life, follow these steps:

1. **Start Small**: Keystone habits don't need to be grand or complex. Begin by identifying small, manageable behaviors that you can implement consistently. These small actions, when repeated regularly, can lead to significant changes over time.
2. **Focus on Consistency**: The key to developing keystone habits is consistency. Choose habits that you can incorporate into your daily routine and commit to practicing them regularly. Over time, these habits will become automatic, creating a ripple effect of positive change.
3. **Track Progress**: Keep track of your progress to stay motivated and accountable. Journaling, habit tracking apps, or simply checking off daily accomplishments can help you stay on track and recognize the impact your keystone habits are having on other areas of your life.
4. **Be Patient**: Keystone habits take time to produce noticeable results. Be patient with yourself and trust the process. The compounding effects of small, positive habits will become evident as you continue to practice them consistently.

Keystone habits are small but powerful behaviors that can create a ripple effect of positive changes in various areas of life. By identifying and cultivating these habits, you can unlock a path to improved health, productivity, emotional well-being, and overall success. Whether it's regular exercise, meditation, journaling, or establishing better sleep hygiene, focusing on keystone habits allows you to harness the power of incremental progress and transform your life one step at a time.

A Step-by-Step Guide to Identifying Your Own Keystone Habits

Identifying keystone habits is a powerful strategy for creating positive, lasting change in your life. These foundational habits not only improve your behavior in one area but also trigger a ripple effect that enhances other aspects of your life. The challenge, however, lies in recognizing which habits have the potential to create this broad, positive impact. In this guide, we'll walk you through the process of identifying your own keystone habits, so you can start building momentum towards a healthier, happier, and more productive life.

Step 1: Reflect on Your Goals and Values

The first step in identifying your keystone habits is to reflect on your **goals** and **values**. What are the key areas of your life that you want to improve? What long-term goals do you want to achieve? And what values are most important to you?

Start by thinking about the major domains of your life, such as:

Health and Fitness: Do you want to lose weight, build strength, or improve your overall well-being?
Career and Productivity: Are you looking to advance in your

career, be more productive, or improve your skills?
Emotional and Mental Health: Do you want to reduce stress, improve your emotional resilience, or enhance your overall happiness?
Relationships and Social Connections: Are you looking to deepen your relationships with family and friends, or build new connections?

Reflect on these areas and ask yourself which are most important to you right now. By aligning your habits with your goals and values, you're more likely to stay motivated and committed to cultivating them.

For example, if your primary goal is to improve your health, keystone habits related to exercise, nutrition, and sleep might be a good fit. If your goal is to advance in your career, habits related to time management, focus, and skill development could be key.

Step 2: Observe Your Current Habits

Once you have a clearer sense of your goals and values, it's time to observe your **current habits**. This step involves identifying which of your existing behaviors might already be functioning as keystone habits, as well as recognizing negative habits that could be holding you back.

Start by asking yourself the following questions:

What habits do I already practice regularly? Think about your daily routines. Do you have any habits that have become automatic, like brushing your teeth, exercising, or checking your email first thing in the morning?
   Which habits contribute positively to my life? Identify the habits that make you feel good or help you achieve your goals. These could be small habits, like drinking a glass of water first thing in the morning, or more substantial ones, like spending time planning your day.

Which habits might be negatively affecting me? Reflect on any negative habits that might be detracting from your goals. For instance, are you spending too much time on social media or procrastinating on important tasks?

By becoming aware of your existing habits, both positive and negative, you can start to identify patterns that either support or hinder your progress.

Step 3: Identify Potential Keystone Habits

Now that you've reflected on your goals and observed your current habits, it's time to identify which of these habits (or new ones) could serve as keystone habits. To do this, consider the following criteria:

1. **Does this habit create a ripple effect?** Keystone habits are those that have the potential to influence other areas of your life. For example, exercise is a keystone habit because it not only improves physical health but also boosts mood, energy, and even productivity. Similarly, getting a good night's sleep can enhance your focus, decision-making, and emotional resilience.
2. **Is this habit small but impactful?** Keystone habits don't need to be grand or difficult to implement. In fact, the most effective keystone habits are often simple and easy to maintain. Small habits, like making your bed every morning or spending five minutes planning your day, can set the tone for the rest of your day and lead to larger positive changes.
3. **Does this habit align with my goals and values?** For a habit to be truly transformative, it should align with your long-term goals and values. For example, if your goal is to improve your health, a keystone habit like exercising regularly or eating a nutritious breakfast might be key. If your goal is to improve your productivity, a keystone habit like setting daily

priorities or practicing mindfulness could help.
4. **Can this habit be built into my routine?** Keystone habits should be easy to integrate into your daily life. They should fit naturally into your existing routines, rather than requiring drastic changes to your schedule. This makes them easier to maintain in the long term.

Consider experimenting with a few different habits to see which ones have the greatest positive impact. For example, if you're unsure whether exercise or meditation will work best as a keystone habit, try implementing both for a few weeks and observe the effects on your life.

Step 4: Test and Refine Your Keystone Habits

Once you've identified potential keystone habits, it's important to **test** them in your daily life. Choose one or two habits to focus on and commit to practicing them consistently for a set period of time (e.g., 30 days). During this period, observe the effects these habits have on other areas of your life.

For example, if you choose exercise as a keystone habit, pay attention to how it influences your mood, energy levels, eating habits, and productivity. If you find that exercising regularly helps you eat healthier, sleep better, and feel more focused at work, then you've likely identified a powerful keystone habit.

Similarly, if you decide to practice gratitude journaling, observe how this habit affects your emotional well-being and relationships. Does it help you feel more positive and connected to others? If so, it might be worth continuing.

As you test your keystone habits, it's important to be flexible and open to refinement. If a habit isn't producing the desired results, consider tweaking it or experimenting with a different habit. For example, if exercising in the evening is difficult to maintain, try switching to a morning workout routine. The goal is to find habits that not only stick but also create positive ripple effects in your life.

Step 5: Build Consistency and Momentum

Once you've identified and tested your keystone habits, the next step is to **build consistency** and **momentum**. The key to making any habit stick is repetition and perseverance. Keystone habits are no different—by practicing them consistently, you allow them to take root and become automatic parts of your routine.

To build consistency, consider using the following strategies:

Start small: Begin with small, manageable versions of your keystone habits. For example, if you've chosen exercise as a keystone habit, start with just 10 minutes a day. As the habit becomes more ingrained, you can gradually increase the duration or intensity.

    Track your progress: Use a habit tracker or journal to record your progress. Tracking helps you stay accountable and provides a sense of accomplishment as you see your streaks grow.

Celebrate small wins: Acknowledge and celebrate your progress along the way. Celebrating small wins reinforces your commitment to the habit and helps build positive momentum.

    Stay flexible: Life is unpredictable, and sometimes your routine will be disrupted. The key is to stay flexible and get back on track as soon as possible. If you miss a day or fall off course, don't be discouraged—just start again the next day.

Identifying your own keystone habits is a powerful way to create lasting change in your life. By reflecting on your goals, observing your current habits, and testing new behaviors, you can discover which habits have the potential to create positive ripple effects across multiple areas of your life. Once identified, these habits can serve as the foundation for your personal growth and success, helping you build momentum toward a healthier, happier, and more productive future.

The key is to start small, stay consistent, and be patient with yourself as you work to integrate these keystone habits into your daily routine. With time and dedication, these habits will become second nature, creating lasting change that extends far beyond the habit itself.

Case Studies of Keystone Habits in Action

Keystone habits are powerful because they don't just change one part of our lives—they have a cascading effect, positively impacting various areas. Below are several case studies that illustrate how keystone habits have transformed individuals' lives in significant and multifaceted ways.

Case Study 1: Charles Duhigg and Exercise as a Keystone Habit

In his book *The Power of Habit*, **Charles Duhigg** discusses the concept of keystone habits and shares the story of **Lisa Allen**, a woman who transformed her life through the keystone habit of exercise.

Lisa had struggled for years with smoking, obesity, and chronic financial problems. Her life was in disarray until she decided to make one significant change: quitting smoking and replacing it with exercise. Exercise became her keystone habit, and over time, it produced a ripple effect throughout her life. As she built the habit of exercising regularly, several other positive changes followed naturally:

Improved Health: As Lisa began exercising, she started eating healthier foods to fuel her workouts. This change improved her physical health and helped her lose weight.

Increased Self-Discipline: The discipline Lisa developed through exercise spread to other areas of her life. She became more organized, started budgeting her money better, and eventually paid off her debts.

  Emotional Resilience: Exercise also helped Lisa manage stress and improve her emotional health. With the added confidence and emotional stability, she repaired strained relationships and improved her work performance.

This case illustrates how exercise, a seemingly simple habit, can lead to significant improvements in multiple areas, including physical health, emotional well-being, finances, and relationships. Lisa's story exemplifies the transformative power of keystone habits, particularly when they are built and maintained over time.

Case Study 2: Benjamin Franklin and Daily Planning as a Keystone Habit

Benjamin Franklin, one of America's Founding Fathers, is often cited as a prime example of how daily planning can function as a keystone habit. Franklin's famous "13 virtues" and meticulous daily schedule exemplified his belief in the importance of self-discipline and planning.

Each day, Franklin followed a strict routine, which began with a question: "What good shall I do today?" He would plan his day in the morning, identifying tasks and goals aligned with his long-term vision. At the end of the day, he would reflect on his actions, asking, "What good have I done today?"

This simple habit of daily planning acted as a keystone habit that enabled Franklin to achieve extraordinary things throughout his life:

  Enhanced Productivity: Franklin's commitment to daily planning helped him stay focused on his tasks and goals, allowing him to balance his time effectively between his many roles as a statesman, inventor, writer, and scientist.

  Self-Improvement: By regularly reflecting on his day, Franklin constantly assessed his progress and adjusted his actions. This habit helped him continually improve and work towards becoming the person he aspired to be.

Character Building: Franklin's habit of daily reflection reinforced his adherence to his 13 virtues, fostering personal growth and integrity. This habit also had a broader impact on his relationships and reputation, helping him cultivate a sense of trustworthiness and reliability.

Franklin's case demonstrates how the keystone habit of daily planning can promote self-discipline, productivity, and personal development, serving as a foundation for success across many areas of life.

Case Study 3: Michael Phelps and Visualization as a Keystone Habit

Michael Phelps, the most decorated Olympian in history, is a powerful example of how visualization and mental preparation can function as a keystone habit. From a young age, Phelps worked closely with his coach, **Bob Bowman**, to develop the habit of visualization as part of his daily routine.

Before every race, Phelps would spend time mentally rehearsing his performance. He would visualize every stroke, every turn, and even how he would react to potential challenges like a bad start or water in his goggles. This habit of mental rehearsal helped him become one of the most successful athletes in the world.

The keystone habit of visualization had several ripple effects on Phelps' performance:

Peak Performance: Visualization allowed Phelps to consistently perform at his best, even under intense pressure. By rehearsing his races mentally, he could anticipate and overcome obstacles before they even happened, leading to extraordinary consistency in competition.

Emotional Regulation: The habit of visualization helped Phelps remain calm and composed, even in high-stakes situations like the Olympics. This emotional control gave him a competitive edge, allowing him to stay focused when others might falter.

Confidence and Resilience: By visualizing successful outcomes repeatedly, Phelps built unshakable confidence in his abilities. This confidence helped him bounce back from setbacks and maintain his competitive spirit throughout his career.

Phelps' story illustrates how a keystone habit like visualization can enhance performance, emotional control, and resilience, leading to long-term success in highly competitive environments.

Case Study 4: Marie Kondo and Decluttering as a Keystone Habit

Marie Kondo, the Japanese organizing consultant and author of *The Life-Changing Magic of Tidying Up*, has built her entire philosophy around the keystone habit of decluttering. Kondo's method, known as the KonMari Method, involves systematically tidying one's living space by keeping only the items that "spark joy" and discarding the rest.

Kondo's own life and the lives of her clients have been transformed by this habit of decluttering:

Mental Clarity and Focus: Decluttering helps individuals clear not only their physical space but also their mental space. By eliminating unnecessary items, people create an environment that fosters clarity, focus, and peace of mind.

Emotional Well-Being: The act of decluttering can also be emotionally liberating, as it encourages individuals to let go of attachments to the past and focus on the present. This emotional release often leads to greater happiness and contentment.

Improved Relationships: Many of Kondo's clients report that decluttering has had a positive impact on their relationships.

By creating a more organized and peaceful home environment, individuals experience less stress and tension, which in turn leads to better communication and stronger connections with loved ones.

Marie Kondo's work highlights how decluttering can act as a keystone habit, leading to improvements in mental clarity, emotional health, and interpersonal relationships. By creating a more organized and intentional living space, individuals are better equipped to pursue their goals and live more fulfilling lives.

Case Study 5: Oprah Winfrey and Gratitude as a Keystone Habit

Oprah Winfrey, media mogul and philanthropist, has long practiced gratitude as a keystone habit. Winfrey has credited her habit of keeping a gratitude journal with transforming her outlook on life. Each day, she writes down five things she is grateful for, no matter how small or simple.

This habit of focusing on gratitude has had a profound impact on Winfrey's life:

Increased Happiness: By regularly practicing gratitude, Winfrey has cultivated a more positive mindset. This shift in perspective has helped her maintain emotional balance and happiness, even in the face of challenges.

Improved Resilience: The habit of gratitude has also strengthened Winfrey's resilience. By focusing on the positive aspects of her life, she is better able to navigate difficulties and setbacks with grace and optimism.

Enhanced Relationships: Gratitude has positively influenced Winfrey's relationships by fostering empathy, appreciation, and kindness. By focusing on what she is thankful for in others, Winfrey has strengthened her connections and built more meaningful relationships.

Oprah's case shows how the keystone habit of gratitude can lead to a more positive, resilient, and connected life. By consistently practicing gratitude, individuals can shift their mindset and create a ripple effect of positivity that touches every area of their lives.

These case studies highlight the transformative power of keystone habits. Whether it's exercise, daily planning, visualization, decluttering, or gratitude, keystone habits can create a domino effect, leading to improvements in multiple areas of life. The key is to identify the habits that resonate with your goals and values, practice them consistently, and allow them to take root in your daily routine.

Keystone habits work because they align with who we want to be and gradually reshape our behaviors and mindsets to support that identity. By focusing on cultivating these foundational habits, you can unlock significant, lasting change in your life—just like Lisa Allen, Benjamin Franklin, Michael Phelps, Marie Kondo, and Oprah Winfrey have done.

CHAPTER 3: CRAFTING YOUR HABIT BLUEPRINT

How to Design a Step-by-Step Habit Blueprint for Success

Designing a **habit blueprint** is a powerful way to systematically build habits that lead to success. A habit blueprint provides a clear, step-by-step framework to help you create, sustain, and ultimately benefit from new habits that align with your goals. Whether you're looking to improve your health, boost your productivity, or enhance your personal growth, a habit blueprint offers a strategic approach to achieving lasting change.

In this guide, we'll walk you through the process of designing your own habit blueprint. By following these steps, you'll be able to establish effective habits, overcome obstacles, and create a foundation for success.

Step 1: Define Your Why

Before diving into the specific habits you want to build, it's crucial to start with **why**. Why do you want to develop these habits? What goals or values do they align with? Understanding your deeper motivations will provide you with the drive and focus needed to sustain your habits over time.

Action Step: Reflect on your long-term goals and values. Ask yourself:

What do I want to achieve in the next 6 months or year?
Why are these goals important to me?
How will building certain habits help me achieve these goals?

For example, if your goal is to improve your health, your "why" might be to feel more energized, reduce stress, or prevent future health issues. Having a clear sense of purpose will help you stay committed to your habits, even when challenges arise.

Step 2: Identify Keystone Habits

Keystone habits are the habits that have the most significant impact on your life. These habits serve as the foundation for building other positive behaviors and can create a ripple effect of change. Your habit blueprint should focus on these powerful habits that align with your goals.

Action Step: Identify 1-3 keystone habits that will drive your success. These could include:

 Exercise: Regular physical activity that boosts your energy, mood, and overall health.
 Daily Planning: A habit of setting goals and priorities each day to improve focus and productivity.
Gratitude Journaling: Writing down three things you are grateful for each day to foster a positive mindset.

Choose keystone habits that are directly connected to your larger goals. For instance, if you want to improve your productivity, daily planning might be a key habit. If your goal is emotional well-being, gratitude journaling could be transformative.

Step 3: Break Down Your Habits into Actionable Steps

Once you've identified your keystone habits, the next step is to break them down into **small, actionable steps**. Big changes can feel overwhelming, but when you break a habit into smaller components, it becomes much easier to implement and maintain.

Action Step: Define the smallest possible action you can take to start your habit. For example:

If your keystone habit is exercise, your smallest action might be

doing 5 minutes of stretching every morning.
If your keystone habit is daily planning, you might start by spending 3 minutes each evening writing down your top 3 priorities for the next day.

By starting with small, manageable actions, you make it easier to establish consistency. Over time, as the habit becomes ingrained, you can gradually increase the intensity or duration.

Step 4: Create a Habit Loop (Cue, Routine, Reward)

The habit loop is the neurological cycle that governs habit formation. It consists of three components: the **cue** (trigger), the **routine** (behavior), and the **reward** (benefit). To successfully build a new habit, you need to design this loop intentionally.

Action Step: For each habit, define the following:

Cue: What will trigger the habit? This could be a specific time of day, a location, or an event. For example, your cue for exercising might be waking up in the morning, or your cue for daily planning might be finishing dinner.
Routine: What specific action will you take? This is the habit itself, such as going for a 10-minute walk or writing in your journal.
Reward: What reward will you give yourself after completing the habit? The reward reinforces the habit and makes it more likely that you'll repeat it. For example, after exercising, you might reward yourself with a relaxing shower or after planning your day, you might enjoy a cup of tea.

Designing your habit loop ensures that your brain recognizes and remembers the pattern, making it easier to build and maintain the habit over time.

Step 5: Establish Accountability and Tracking

Accountability is a crucial factor in habit formation. It helps ensure that you stay consistent and motivated. Additionally, tracking your progress can reinforce your commitment and provide a sense of accomplishment as you see your habits take shape.

Action Step:

Accountability: Share your habit goals with someone you trust, such as a friend, family member, or coach. You might also join a group or community where others are working on similar habits.
Tracking: Use a habit tracker, journal, or app to track your progress. Each day, mark off when you complete your habit. Tracking helps you stay focused and motivated, especially during the early stages when the habit is still forming.

For example, you could create a simple habit tracker where you check off each day that you complete your habit, or you could use an app like Habitica or Streaks to keep track of your progress digitally.

Step 6: Anticipate Obstacles and Plan for Them

No matter how well you design your habit blueprint, obstacles are inevitable. Life gets busy, motivation wanes, and unexpected challenges arise. The key to sustaining your habits is to anticipate these obstacles and develop strategies to overcome them.

Action Step: Identify potential obstacles for each habit and create a plan to address them. For example:

Obstacle: You might feel too tired to exercise after a long day of work.

Plan: To overcome this, you could schedule your workouts for the morning, before your energy levels dip, or choose a low-intensity workout on particularly busy days.

By planning for setbacks in advance, you're less likely to be derailed when they occur. Have a backup plan ready so that even if you can't complete your habit perfectly, you can still make progress.

Step 7: Build Flexibility into Your Habits

While consistency is important, so is flexibility. Life is unpredictable, and there will be days when you can't stick to your routine exactly as planned. The key is to allow for flexibility without completely abandoning the habit.

Action Step: Create a "minimum viable habit" for days when you're short on time or energy. For example:

On busy days, your minimum viable habit for exercise might be doing 5 squats or taking a short walk around the block.

For daily planning, you might spend just 1 minute jotting down your top priority for the day instead of a full plan.

Having a reduced version of your habit ensures that you maintain the momentum, even when circumstances aren't ideal.

Step 8: Reflect and Adjust

Regular reflection allows you to evaluate the effectiveness of your habits and make adjustments as needed. As you progress, your needs and goals may evolve, and your habits should adapt accordingly.

Action Step: Schedule regular check-ins (e.g., weekly or monthly) to reflect on your progress. Ask yourself:

How consistent have I been with my habits?
What positive effects have I noticed as a result of these habits?
Are there any adjustments I need to make to improve my routine?

Use these reflections to fine-tune your habit blueprint. If you notice certain habits aren't having the desired effect, don't be afraid to tweak them or try new strategies.

Step 9: Celebrate Your Wins

Celebrating your successes, no matter how small, reinforces your commitment to your habits and boosts your motivation to continue. Acknowledging progress helps you stay focused on the bigger picture and keeps you engaged in the process.

Action Step: Create milestones to celebrate as you achieve them. For example, after 30 consecutive days of sticking to a habit, reward yourself with something special, like a day off, a favorite meal, or a small gift.

Celebrating your wins, both big and small, helps you associate positive emotions with your habits, making it more likely that you'll stick with them in the long term.

Designing a habit blueprint for success involves breaking down your goals into actionable steps, building a habit loop, establishing accountability, and anticipating obstacles. By following these steps, you'll be able to create habits that align with your goals, fit into your life, and generate lasting positive changes.

Remember, the key to habit success is consistency, patience, and adaptability. With your habit blueprint in hand, you'll have a clear path toward building the habits that will ultimately lead you to the life you want to live.

Templates and Examples for Daily Routines

Creating a daily routine is a powerful way to build consistency and achieve success across various areas of your life. A well-structured routine helps you prioritize your most important tasks, establish healthy habits, and maximize your productivity. In this section, we'll provide templates and examples for designing effective daily routines that align with your goals, along with tips on how to customize them for your unique needs.

Template 1: Morning Routine for Productivity and Well-Being

The morning sets the tone for the rest of your day, so establishing a strong morning routine can have a profound impact on your productivity and mindset.

Template Example:

Wake Up (6:00 AM): Wake up at the same time every day to regulate your sleep cycle.
Hydrate (6:05 AM): Drink a glass of water to rehydrate your body after a night of sleep.
Morning Exercise (6:10 AM - 6:30 AM): Engage in light physical activity, such as yoga, stretching, or a short workout, to energize your body.
Meditation/Mindfulness (6:30 AM - 6:45 AM): Spend 10-15 minutes meditating or practicing mindfulness to calm your mind and reduce stress.
Breakfast (6:45 AM - 7:00 AM): Eat a nutritious breakfast that includes protein, healthy fats, and fruits or vegetables to fuel your day.
Daily Planning (7:00 AM - 7:15 AM): Write down your top three priorities for the day and any additional tasks you need to accomplish. Use a planner or journal to organize your day.

Personal Development (7:15 AM - 7:30 AM): Spend 15 minutes reading, journaling, or engaging in a hobby that enriches your mind.

Example Morning Routine:

Wake Up: 6:00 AM
Hydrate: Drink a glass of water with lemon.
Exercise: 20 minutes of yoga to stretch and wake up your body.
Meditation: 10 minutes of guided meditation using a mindfulness app.
Breakfast: Scrambled eggs with spinach, avocado, and a slice of whole-grain toast.
Daily Planning: Review your planner and write down the top three tasks for the day.
Personal Development: Read one chapter from a self-development book or spend 15 minutes journaling.

Template 2: Midday Routine for Focus and Productivity

The midday routine is essential for maintaining momentum, staying focused, and preventing burnout. Taking breaks and managing energy levels is crucial for sustained productivity.

Template Example:

Focused Work Block (9:00 AM - 12:00 PM): Begin your most important work tasks for the day. Use the Pomodoro technique (25 minutes of focused work followed by a 5-minute break).
Break/Lunch (12:00 PM - 1:00 PM): Step away from your workspace to have a nutritious lunch and take a mental break. Avoid eating at your desk to fully disconnect.
Walk or Stretch (1:00 PM - 1:15 PM): Engage in a short walk outside or do some light stretching to refresh your body and mind.
Afternoon Work Block (1:15 PM - 4:00 PM): Continue working on tasks. Schedule meetings or collaborative work during this time if needed.

Mini-Mindfulness Break (3:00 PM - 3:05 PM): Take 5 minutes to practice deep breathing or quick meditation to reset your focus.

Example Midday Routine:

Focused Work Block: 9:00 AM - 12:00 PM; Use the Pomodoro technique for focused work on a project.
Lunch: 12:00 PM; Eat a balanced meal like a quinoa salad with grilled chicken and vegetables.
Walk: 1:00 PM; Take a 15-minute walk around the neighborhood for fresh air.
Afternoon Work Block: 1:15 PM - 4:00 PM; Respond to emails, attend meetings, and complete additional tasks.
Mini-Mindfulness Break: 3:00 PM; Take 5 minutes to close your eyes and focus on your breathing.

Template 3: Evening Routine for Wind-Down and Reflection

The evening routine is about unwinding from the day, preparing for a good night's sleep, and setting yourself up for success the next day.

Template Example:

Unplug from Work (6:00 PM): Finish any remaining work and set boundaries to separate work from personal time.
Dinner and Relaxation (6:30 PM - 7:30 PM): Enjoy a healthy dinner and engage in relaxing activities, such as reading, watching a show, or spending time with family.
Reflection and Gratitude Journaling (7:30 PM - 7:45 PM): Reflect on your day by writing down three things you're grateful for and reviewing what went well and what can be improved.
Plan for Tomorrow (7:45 PM - 8:00 PM): Look at your schedule for the next day and set your priorities.
Wind Down (8:00 PM - 9:30 PM): Engage in a calming routine to signal to your body that it's time to sleep. This can include activities like reading, taking a warm bath, or practicing

relaxation techniques.

Bedtime (9:30 PM): Aim for a consistent bedtime to ensure you get 7-8 hours of sleep each night.

Example Evening Routine:

Unplug from Work: 6:00 PM; Shut down your computer and avoid checking work emails.
Dinner: 6:30 PM; Eat a balanced dinner with vegetables and lean protein.
Relaxation: 7:00 PM; Watch a favorite TV show or read a fiction book.
Gratitude Journaling: 7:30 PM; Write down three things you're grateful for and review your accomplishments for the day.
Plan for Tomorrow: 7:45 PM; Review tomorrow's schedule and set goals.
Wind Down: 8:00 PM; Take a warm bath and spend time reading in bed.
Bedtime: 9:30 PM; Lights off for a full night of sleep.

Template 4: Customizable Daily Routine

This template allows for more flexibility and customization. You can adapt it to your specific needs, focusing on different priorities such as work, personal development, or family time.

Template Example:

Morning Block (6:00 AM - 9:00 AM): Morning routine (exercise, breakfast, planning).
Work Block 1 (9:00 AM - 12:00 PM): Focused work tasks or study.
Break (12:00 PM - 1:00 PM): Lunch and relaxation.
Work Block 2 (1:00 PM - 3:00 PM): Continued work or creative projects.
Afternoon Break (3:00 PM - 3:30 PM): Relaxation or short walk.
Personal Development Block (3:30 PM - 5:00 PM): Focus on learning, hobbies, or self-improvement.
Evening Block (5:00 PM - 10:00 PM): Wind down, spend time

with family, dinner, and relaxation.

Example Customizable Routine:

Morning Block: 6:00 AM; Wake up, meditate for 10 minutes, eat a light breakfast, and review the day's tasks.
Work Block 1: 9:00 AM - 12:00 PM; Focus on project work or professional tasks.
Break: 12:00 PM; Lunch and a quick walk outside to refresh.
Work Block 2: 1:00 PM - 3:00 PM; Continue with work, respond to emails, or have meetings.
Personal Development Block: 3:30 PM - 5:00 PM; Work on a personal passion project, read a book, or practice a new skill.
Evening Block: 5:00 PM; Have dinner, watch TV, and spend time with family or relax before bed.

Daily routines are the foundation of success, and by establishing them through well-planned templates, you can create habits that positively impact your health, productivity, and overall well-being. These templates are just starting points—feel free to customize them based on your specific goals and lifestyle. Whether you prioritize morning rituals for productivity, midday breaks for focus, or evening routines for winding down, a well-structured routine can help you make the most out of each day.

How to Set Achievable Goals and Plan for Habit Formation

Goal-setting and habit formation are two interdependent processes that are fundamental to achieving long-term success. Goals provide direction and motivation, while habits are the consistent actions that propel you toward those goals. To ensure lasting change, it's essential to set realistic, achievable goals and plan for habit formation in a way that is sustainable and effective. In this section, we'll explore how to set achievable goals and develop habits that support them.

Step 1: Define Clear and Specific Goals

The first step in achieving your goals is to clearly define them. Vague or overly ambitious goals often lead to frustration and failure, so it's important to be specific about what you want to accomplish. A proven method for goal-setting is the **SMART** framework, which ensures that your goals are well-defined and achievable.

SMART Goals are:

Specific: Clearly define what you want to accomplish. Avoid vague language.
Measurable: Make sure you can track your progress and measure your success.
Achievable: Set realistic goals that are within your reach, given your current resources and circumstances.
Relevant: Ensure your goals are aligned with your values and long-term object   **Time-bound**: Set a deadline for achieving your goals to create a sense of urgency.

Example of a SMART Goal: Instead of setting a vague goal like, "I want to get fit," you could set a SMART goal: "I want to lose 10 pounds in the next three months by exercising for 30 minutes five days a week and eating a balanced diet."

This goal is specific (losing 10 pounds), measurable (you can track your weight), achievable (within the realm of possibility for most people), relevant (it aligns with the desire for better health), and time-bound (three months).

Step 2: Break Goals Down into Actionable Steps

Once you've defined your goals, break them down into smaller, actionable steps. Large goals can feel overwhelming, but when you divide them into manageable tasks, they become more achievable. Each small step should bring you closer to your overall goal.

Actionable Steps Example: For the goal of losing 10 pounds in three months, your actionable steps might look like this:

Week 1: Start with 20-minute walks after dinner three times a week.
Week 2: Increase walks to 30 minutes, five times a week.
Week 3: Incorporate one session of strength training per week.
Week 4: Add an additional strength training session and increase water intake to eight glasses a day.

Breaking your goal into weekly or daily steps makes it easier to build momentum and stay consistent.

Step 3: Identify Keystone Habits

As discussed earlier, keystone habits are habits that have a positive ripple effect on other areas of your life. Identifying keystone habits that support your goals is a powerful way to ensure success.

For example, if your goal is to lose weight, regular exercise might be a keystone habit that also encourages better eating habits, improved sleep, and reduced stress. Once you've identified your keystone habits, you can focus on developing them first, knowing that they will positively impact other areas of your life.

Keystone Habit Example: For the goal of improving productivity, a keystone habit might be planning your day the night before. This habit sets you up for a more organized and focused day, which can improve time management, reduce procrastination, and help you accomplish more.

Step 4: Use Habit Stacking to Build New Habits

One effective strategy for habit formation is **habit stacking**, which involves attaching a new habit to an existing one. By linking a new habit to something you already do regularly, you make it easier to incorporate the new behavior into your routine.

Habit Stacking Example: If you want to start meditating daily but struggle to find the time, you could stack it onto an existing habit. For example, after you brush your teeth in the morning, you could meditate for five minutes. Since brushing your teeth is already a well-established habit, attaching meditation to this routine increases the likelihood that the new habit will stick.

Habit stacking relies on the strength of your existing habits to reinforce new ones, making it a powerful tool for habit formation.

Step 5: Make Your Habits Specific and Easy to Start

When forming new habits, it's crucial to make them as specific and easy as possible, especially in the beginning. Trying to implement a large or vague habit can lead to resistance and frustration. Instead, focus on small, specific habits that are easy to complete.

Example of a Specific and Easy Habit: If your goal is to read more books, start with the habit of reading just two pages a day. This is specific, actionable, and so easy that it feels almost impossible to skip. Once the habit is established, you can gradually increase the amount of time you spend reading.

By lowering the barrier to entry, you're more likely to get started and build consistency. Over time, as the habit becomes ingrained, you can expand it to achieve greater results.

Step 6: Track Your Progress

Tracking your progress is a vital part of both goal-setting and habit formation. It allows you to see how far you've come and keeps you accountable to your commitments. Tracking also provides motivation, as each small success builds confidence and momentum.

Habit Tracking Example: You can use a habit tracker, journal, or mobile app to record your progress. For example, if your goal is to exercise five times a week, you can mark off each day you complete your workout. Seeing a streak of completed days can motivate you to keep going.

Tracking progress also helps you identify patterns and areas where you might need to adjust your habits. If you notice you consistently miss workouts on Fridays, for example, you might need to find a more convenient time or adjust your routine for that day.

Step 7: Plan for Obstacles

No matter how well you plan, obstacles will arise. The key to overcoming these challenges is to anticipate them in advance and develop strategies for dealing with them. By planning for obstacles, you reduce the likelihood that they will derail your progress.

Common Obstacles and Solutions:

Obstacle: Lack of time due to a busy schedule.
Solution: Identify small pockets of time throughout the day where you can fit in your habit, such as a 10-minute walk during lunch or a quick morning meditation.
Obstacle: Low motivation on certain days.
Solution: Create a "minimum viable habit" for low-motivation days. For example, if you're not feeling up to a full workout, commit to doing just 5 minutes of stretching.
Obstacle: Disruptions in routine, such as travel or unexpected events.
Solution: Develop a flexible version of your habit that can be done anywhere. If you travel frequently, find a portable exercise routine or meditation app that you can use on the go.

By having a plan in place for common obstacles, you can

maintain consistency even when life gets in the way.

Step 8: Celebrate Small Wins and Adjust as Needed

Celebrating your successes, no matter how small, reinforces your habit and provides positive reinforcement. Recognizing your achievements helps build confidence and keeps you motivated to continue.

Celebrate Small Wins Example: Set milestones for your goals and celebrate when you reach them. For instance, if your goal is to write a book, celebrate after completing each chapter. These celebrations don't need to be extravagant—a simple reward like a favorite treat or an extra hour of relaxation can suffice.

At the same time, be open to adjusting your habits and goals as needed. Life circumstances may change, or you may discover new strategies that work better for you. Flexibility is key to long-term success.

Step 9: Create a Long-Term Vision

While short-term goals and habits are important, it's also helpful to connect them to a larger, long-term vision. Understanding how your current efforts fit into your broader life goals can help you stay motivated and committed.

Example of a Long-Term Vision: If your goal is to become healthier, your long-term vision might be to live a long, active life, free from chronic illness. Every healthy meal you eat and every workout you complete contributes to this vision, reinforcing the importance of your daily habits.

Connecting your habits to a long-term vision helps you stay focused on the bigger picture, even when progress feels slow or incremental.

Setting achievable goals and planning for habit formation

are essential steps in creating lasting change. By using the SMART framework to define your goals, breaking them down into actionable steps, identifying keystone habits, and using strategies like habit stacking, you can build habits that support your success.

Remember to make your habits easy to start, track your progress, plan for obstacles, and celebrate your wins along the way. With patience, persistence, and a clear vision, you'll be well on your way to achieving your goals and creating the life you desire.

CHAPTER 4: THE POWER OF SMALL WINS

The Importance of Celebrating Small Victories to Maintain Motivation

Achieving goals and maintaining motivation can be challenging, especially when the path to success seems long and arduous. One of the most effective ways to sustain motivation over time is by celebrating small victories. These incremental wins not only provide positive reinforcement but also help break the journey into manageable steps, making the larger goal feel more achievable. Whether you're trying to establish new habits, reach personal milestones, or pursue a long-term project, acknowledging and celebrating small victories can make all the difference in keeping you engaged and on track.

Why Small Victories Matter

1. They Build Momentum

Small victories act as stepping stones that propel you toward your larger goal. Each time you achieve a small win, you gain a sense of progress that builds momentum. This momentum is essential because it keeps you moving forward, even when the end goal seems distant.

Consider the analogy of climbing a mountain. The peak may seem far off, but every step you take brings you closer. If you only focus on how far you are from the summit, it's easy to get discouraged. However, if you take the time to celebrate reaching a new elevation or a scenic viewpoint along the way, you reinforce the progress you've made and boost your motivation to keep going.

2. They Provide Positive Reinforcement

From a psychological perspective, small victories serve as powerful forms of positive reinforcement. When you acknowledge and celebrate your achievements, your brain releases dopamine, a neurotransmitter associated with pleasure and reward. This dopamine release makes you feel good, reinforcing the behavior that led to the win and increasing the likelihood that you'll repeat that behavior in the future.

For example, if you're working on a fitness goal and celebrate completing your first week of consistent workouts, your brain associates the act of working out with the positive feeling of accomplishment. This makes you more likely to stick with your exercise routine in the long run.

3. They Create a Positive Feedback Loop

Small victories help establish a positive feedback loop where progress fuels motivation, and motivation drives further progress. By consistently celebrating small wins, you create a cycle of success that builds upon itself. Each achievement, no matter how minor, reinforces the belief that you are capable of reaching your larger goal, which, in turn, motivates you to keep pushing forward.

This feedback loop is particularly valuable in habit formation. When you celebrate small wins related to your new habits, you create a sense of reward and satisfaction that makes it easier to continue practicing the habit until it becomes ingrained.

How Celebrating Small Victories Improves Habit Formation

Establishing new habits requires consistency and patience. Unfortunately, many people abandon new habits prematurely because they don't see immediate results or feel that their progress is too slow. Celebrating small victories helps counteract this tendency by giving you tangible milestones to acknowledge along the way, which keeps you motivated during the habit formation process.

1. Increases Consistency

Consistency is the key to habit formation, and celebrating small victories encourages you to stay consistent. Each time you achieve a small milestone, you reaffirm your commitment to the habit, making it easier to continue. For example, if you're trying to develop the habit of drinking more water, celebrating when you successfully hit your daily water intake for a week reinforces the behavior, making you more likely to continue.

2. Reduces the Pressure of Perfection

Celebrating small victories helps shift your focus away from perfection and toward progress. When you celebrate incremental achievements, you recognize that you don't need to be perfect every day to succeed in building a habit. This reduces the pressure and allows you to view slip-ups as part of the process rather than as failures.

For instance, if your goal is to write every day and you miss a day or two, focusing on the days you did write (and celebrating those) keeps you motivated to get back on track rather than giving up altogether.

3. Strengthens the Habit Loop

As discussed earlier, habits are formed through a loop of cue, routine, and reward. Celebrating small victories serves as the reward component of this loop, which reinforces the habit. When you reward yourself for completing a habit, you create a strong association between the behavior and the positive feelings that come from the reward. Over time, this strengthens the habit and makes it more automatic.

For example, if you're building the habit of exercising in the morning, celebrating each time you complete a workout reinforces the habit. You might treat yourself to a post-workout smoothie or simply acknowledge your accomplishment with a sense of pride. These small rewards help solidify the habit in your daily routine.

The Psychological Benefits of Celebrating Small Victories

In addition to reinforcing habits and building momentum, celebrating small victories has a range of psychological benefits that contribute to overall well-being and sustained motivation.

1. Boosts Confidence and Self-Efficacy

Celebrating small wins boosts your confidence and self-efficacy—the belief in your ability to succeed. Each small victory serves as evidence that you are capable of making progress and achieving your goals. This growing confidence makes you more resilient in the face of challenges and setbacks, as you have a track record of success to draw upon.

For example, if you're learning a new skill like playing an instrument, celebrating small achievements, such as mastering a new chord or playing a simple song, increases your belief that you can eventually reach a higher level of proficiency. This confidence makes you more likely to persevere through difficult learning curves.

2. Enhances Resilience

Celebrating small victories fosters resilience by helping you maintain a positive mindset even when progress is slow. Acknowledging incremental progress teaches you to appreciate the journey rather than just the destination, which makes it easier to stay motivated when you encounter obstacles.

For example, if you're working on a long-term project, such as writing a book, celebrating each chapter you complete helps you stay motivated, even when the overall task feels overwhelming. By focusing on the progress you've made, you're better equipped to handle challenges and setbacks with a resilient attitude.

3. Improves Mental Health

Small victories contribute to better mental health by promoting feelings of accomplishment, reducing stress, and boosting overall happiness. The act of celebrating—even something small—triggers positive emotions that can lift your mood and provide relief from the stress and pressure of pursuing larger goals.

For example, if you're trying to manage stress through mindfulness practice, celebrating each day you successfully meditate for a few minutes reinforces the positive effects of the practice and helps reduce overall stress levels.

How to Celebrate Small Victories Effectively

Celebrating small victories doesn't have to be elaborate or time-consuming. The key is to acknowledge your progress in a meaningful way that resonates with you. Here are some simple ways to celebrate your wins:

1. Keep a Victory Journal Record your small victories in a journal, along with how they made you feel and how they contributed to your larger goal. This practice helps you reflect on your progress and provides a positive reminder of how far you've come.

2. Treat Yourself Reward yourself with a small treat when you reach a milestone. This could be anything from enjoying your favorite snack, taking a relaxing bath, or giving yourself a short break to do something you love.

3. Share Your Wins Share your small victories with a friend, family member, or accountability partner. Celebrating with others amplifies the sense of accomplishment and provides additional encouragement and support.

4. Take a Moment to Reflect Simply take a moment to pause and reflect on your progress. Acknowledge the hard work and effort that went into achieving your small victory, and allow yourself to feel proud of what you've accomplished.

5. Create Visual Reminders Use visual cues to track your progress, such as crossing off days on a calendar, using a habit tracker app, or creating a visual board of your achievements. These reminders reinforce the positive actions you've taken and keep you motivated.

Celebrating small victories is a crucial part of maintaining motivation and building lasting success. These incremental wins create momentum, provide positive reinforcement, and establish a positive feedback loop that makes it easier to stay consistent in your efforts. In addition to reinforcing habits, celebrating small victories boosts confidence, enhances resilience, and improves overall mental health.

By incorporating regular celebrations into your goal-setting and habit formation process, you create a sustainable path to success that acknowledges progress every step of the way. Whether through simple reflection, a small treat, or sharing your wins with others, taking the time to celebrate your achievements ensures that you stay motivated, engaged, and optimistic as you work toward your larger goals.

How Small, Consistent Wins Can Snowball Into Big Changes

In the pursuit of personal growth and success, many people focus on achieving significant milestones or making drastic transformations. However, some of the most profound changes in life come not from one-time actions, but from **small, consistent wins**. These incremental successes accumulate over time and create a snowball effect, leading to substantial, long-term transformations. This concept is rooted in the idea that small actions, when repeated consistently, have the power to generate momentum and compounding effects that result in significant outcomes.

This article explores how small wins, when maintained consistently, can build momentum and lead to major life changes. We will examine the science behind this principle, how it applies in different areas of life, and how you can harness its power to create lasting impact.

The Science Behind Small Wins and the Snowball Effect

The idea that small wins can snowball into bigger changes is supported by the principles of **habit formation**, **compounding effects**, and **psychological momentum**.

1. **Habit Formation**: Small wins are often the result of consistent habits. According to research in behavioral psychology, habits are formed through repetition, where actions become automatic responses to specific cues. As these actions are repeated consistently, they become ingrained in our daily routines, requiring less conscious effort. Over time, these small habitual behaviors compound and lead to larger shifts in behavior and outcomes.
2. **Compounding Effects**: Similar to the way compound interest grows over time, small actions, when consistently applied, lead to exponential growth. For example, improving by just 1% each day might seem insignificant in the moment, but over the course of a year, this improvement can add up to significant progress. The compounding effect means that each small win builds upon the last, leading to larger and more meaningful outcomes.
3. **Psychological Momentum**: Small wins also create psychological momentum, which is the perception that progress is being made. This momentum increases motivation and confidence, making it easier to continue pushing forward. The more small wins

you accumulate, the more motivated you become to tackle larger challenges, as the belief in your ability to succeed strengthens.

How Small Wins Snowball Into Big Changes

The snowball effect of small wins can be seen in various aspects of life, including personal development, career growth, health, and relationships. Let's explore some examples to illustrate how this concept works in practice.

1. Health and Fitness

One of the most common areas where small wins lead to big changes is in health and fitness. Many people set ambitious goals like losing a significant amount of weight, running a marathon, or transforming their physique. While these are admirable goals, they can feel overwhelming if approached all at once.

However, breaking these large goals into small, consistent actions makes them more achievable. For example:

Start Small: Instead of committing to a 60-minute workout every day, you might start with a 10-minute walk. This small, consistent action is easy to implement and sustain.
Build Consistency: As walking becomes a daily habit, you may increase the duration or intensity of your exercise routine. Over time, that initial 10-minute walk can evolve into a 30-minute jog, then into a more structured workout routine.
Snowball Effect: As you continue to exercise consistently, other areas of your health may improve. You may find yourself eating healthier, sleeping better, and feeling more energetic. These cumulative effects result in significant changes in your overall health and fitness.

An example of this snowball effect in action is someone who starts with small dietary changes—such as adding an extra serving of vegetables to one meal a day. Over time, this seemingly small habit may lead to broader changes in eating habits, weight loss, and improved energy levels. The key is that these changes happen gradually but consistently, building upon each other to create a significant transformation.

2. Career and Professional Growth

The same principle applies in the realm of career and professional growth. Achieving big career goals often requires small, consistent efforts over time. Whether it's mastering a new skill, advancing in your job, or building a business, small wins can accumulate into major achievements.

For instance:

Learning and Skill Development: If your goal is to learn a new skill, such as coding or public speaking, you don't need to become an expert overnight. You might start with just 15 minutes of practice each day. Over time, that daily practice compounds, and within a few months, you may have developed a strong foundation in the skill.

Networking and Opportunities: Building professional relationships is another area where small wins snowball into big changes. Sending one email a week to connect with a potential mentor or attending one networking event each month might seem insignificant initially. However, over time, these small actions can lead to new opportunities, collaborations, and career advancements.

Advancement and Success: As you accumulate small wins —whether it's completing a certification course, receiving positive feedback on a project, or building a strong network —you position yourself for larger successes. Each small win builds your confidence, expands your expertise, and brings you closer to achieving your long-term career goals.

3. Personal Development and Growth

In personal development, small wins can lead to profound changes in mindset, confidence, and resilience. The key is to focus on incremental progress rather than trying to achieve instant transformation.

Examples of how small wins lead to personal growth include:

Building Confidence: Small wins build confidence over time. For example, if you're working on improving your public speaking skills, starting with small tasks like speaking up in meetings or presenting to a small group can help build the confidence needed for larger presentations or public speaking engagements.

Developing Resilience: Personal growth often involves overcoming challenges and setbacks. By setting small, manageable goals, you build resilience. Each time you achieve a small win, you reinforce your ability to persevere, making it easier to tackle more significant challenges in the future.

Changing Mindsets: Positive thinking and gratitude are areas where small wins can snowball into significant mental shifts. For example, starting a gratitude practice by writing down three things you're grateful for each day can lead to a more positive outlook on life. Over time, this practice can change the way you approach challenges, relationships, and opportunities.

4. Relationships and Social Connections

In relationships, small, consistent actions can deepen connections and improve communication over time. Whether it's with a partner, family member, or friend, small wins in relationship-building can lead to more meaningful, fulfilling connections.

Examples of how small wins enhance relationships include:

Consistent Effort: Small acts of kindness or appreciation—like sending a thoughtful text, expressing gratitude, or doing something helpful—can strengthen relationships. These actions might seem minor, but when practiced consistently, they build trust, love, and connection over time.

Better Communication: Improving communication within

relationships is often the result of small, consistent efforts to listen better, express feelings more clearly, or address conflicts constructively. These small communication wins can help resolve issues before they escalate and foster deeper understanding between individuals.

Small, consistent wins have the power to snowball into big changes over time. By focusing on incremental progress, building momentum, and reinforcing positive behaviors, you can create lasting transformation in various areas of your life. Whether it's improving your health, advancing in your career, growing personally, or enhancing relationships, the key is to start small, stay consistent, and celebrate each step along the way. The cumulative effect of these small wins will propel you forward, helping you achieve big goals and experience significant growth over time.

Strategies for Tracking Progress and Maintaining Momentum

Tracking your progress and maintaining momentum are crucial elements for achieving any long-term goal or establishing new habits. Without a system to measure progress and ways to stay motivated, it can be easy to lose focus or give up entirely. In this section, we'll explore strategies for tracking your progress effectively and keeping the momentum going so that you can stay committed to your goals over the long haul.

1. Use a Habit Tracker or Journal

One of the most effective ways to track progress is by using a **habit tracker** or journal. A habit tracker provides a visual representation of your consistency, which can be incredibly motivating. Whether in the form of an app, a bullet journal, or a simple calendar, habit trackers allow you to see your daily or weekly efforts and identify patterns in your behavior.

How to Use a Habit Tracker:

Choose Your Format: Decide whether you prefer a digital

tracker, such as an app (e.g., Habitica, Streaks), or a physical one like a bullet journal. Both options have their benefits—digital trackers can send you reminders, while physical trackers provide a tactile sense of accomplishment when you mark off your progress.

Set Specific Metrics: Define what success looks like for each day or week. For example, if your goal is to exercise, your tracker might log the number of minutes spent exercising each day. If you're building a writing habit, it might track word count.

Mark Your Progress: Each time you complete your habit, mark it in your tracker. Over time, seeing a chain of successful days can motivate you to keep going and avoid breaking the streak.

Example:

Create a simple grid with days of the week across the top and habits listed down the side. Each day you complete the habit, fill in the corresponding box. The longer your streak, the more likely you are to keep it going, as breaking the chain can be psychologically disappointing.

2. Break Large Goals Into Smaller Milestones

Large goals can feel overwhelming, but breaking them down into smaller milestones helps you track progress in more manageable chunks. Each milestone represents a small victory, giving you a sense of achievement and keeping your motivation high.

How to Break Goals into Milestones:

Identify Major Steps: Break your goal down into its major components. For example, if your goal is to run a marathon, your milestones might include completing a 5K, 10K, half marathon, and finally, the full marathon.

Set a Timeline: Assign a specific timeline to each milestone to help you stay on track. This creates short-term deadlines that provide a sense of urgency and purpose.

Celebrate Milestones: Each time you reach a milestone,

celebrate the achievement. Whether it's a small reward like treating yourself to a favorite meal or taking a day off to relax, acknowledging your success reinforces your commitment to the overall goal.

Example:

If your goal is to write a 60,000-word novel, break it down into milestones of 10,000 words each. Once you hit each milestone, you might reward yourself with a fun activity or a break. Tracking each milestone builds momentum and makes the larger goal feel more attainable.

3. Reflect on Your Progress Regularly

Reflection is a powerful tool for maintaining momentum because it allows you to evaluate what's working, what's not, and how far you've come. Regularly reviewing your progress helps you stay aligned with your goals and make any necessary adjustments along the way.

How to Reflect on Your Progress:

Schedule Reflection Sessions: Set aside time at the end of each week or month to reflect on your progress. Use this time to review your habit tracker or journal, assess what worked well, and identify areas for improvement.
Ask Reflective Questions: During your reflection sessions, ask yourself questions like:
What progress have I made toward my goal this week/month?
What challenges did I encounter, and how did I overcome them?
Are there any habits or strategies that need to be adjusted?
Document Your Insights: Write down your reflections so you can track patterns over time. This documentation provides valuable insights into your progress and helps you stay motivated by recognizing the cumulative effect of your efforts.

Example:

If you're working toward a fitness goal, reflect at the end of each week on how many workouts you completed, how you felt after each session, and any obstacles you faced (e.g., scheduling conflicts or low energy). Adjust your plan for the following week based on these reflections.

4. Use Visual Reminders and Cues

Visual reminders and cues help keep your goals top of mind and serve as a constant source of motivation. These reminders can take many forms, from sticky notes on your mirror to vision boards or digital wallpapers.

How to Use Visual Reminders:

Create a Vision Board: Collect images and words that represent your goals and put them on a vision board. Place this board somewhere you'll see it daily to keep your motivation high.
Use Sticky Notes: Write motivational quotes or goal reminders on sticky notes and place them in visible areas, such as your bathroom mirror, computer monitor, or refrigerator.
Set Digital Reminders: Set your phone or computer background to an image that reminds you of your goal. Additionally, set reminders or alarms with motivational messages to prompt you to stay on track.

Example:

If your goal is to learn a new language, place sticky notes with vocabulary words around your home or workspace. You might also set a reminder on your phone that pops up daily with an encouraging message, reminding you to study.

5. Reward Yourself for Consistency

Rewards play a crucial role in maintaining momentum because

they provide positive reinforcement. When you reward yourself for sticking to your habits or achieving milestones, you create an association between your efforts and a sense of accomplishment, making it more likely you'll continue.

How to Implement Rewards:

Set Small, Frequent Rewards: Set up small rewards for maintaining short-term consistency. For example, if you stick to your habit for seven days in a row, treat yourself to a small indulgence, like a favorite snack or a relaxing activity.
Create Bigger Rewards for Milestones: Plan larger rewards for achieving significant milestones or long-term consistency. For example, if you stick with your habit for 30 days, reward yourself with a special experience, like a weekend getaway or a new purchase.
Avoid Overindulgence: While rewarding yourself is important, be mindful not to choose rewards that counteract your goals. For instance, if your goal is health-related, avoid using junk food as a reward. Instead, choose rewards that align with your overall objectives.

Example:

If you're working on a creative project, set a reward for completing each section or chapter. After reaching a major milestone, you could reward yourself with a creative break, like visiting a gallery or spending time in nature.

6. Build Accountability Through Others

Accountability is a powerful motivator for staying on track with your goals. When you share your progress with others or work alongside someone with similar goals, you're more likely to follow through because of the added responsibility.

How to Build Accountability:

Find an Accountability Partner: Partner with someone who is working on a similar goal, and check in with each other regularly. Share your progress, challenges, and wins. Knowing that someone else is counting on you can keep you motivated.
Join a Group or Community: Many people find motivation in joining a community or group where members share their goals and provide mutual support. This could be a fitness class, an online group, or a mastermind circle.
Share Your Goals Publicly: Sharing your goals with friends, family, or on social media can create external accountability. When others know what you're working toward, it can increase your commitment to following through.

Example:

If your goal is to write a book, you could join a writing group where members meet weekly to discuss their progress, exchange feedback, and hold each other accountable. Knowing that you have a scheduled check-in helps keep you on track.

7. Focus on the Process, Not Just the Outcome

Focusing on the process rather than the outcome helps you stay engaged and motivated, even when progress toward the larger goal feels slow. By shifting your attention to the daily actions and habits that will eventually lead to success, you reduce the pressure to achieve immediate results and build momentum over time.

How to Focus on the Process:

Set Process-Oriented Goals: Instead of focusing solely on the end result, set goals based on the actions you can control. For example, rather than setting a goal to "lose 20 pounds," set a goal to "exercise for 30 minutes five times a week."
Celebrate Daily Actions: Acknowledge and celebrate the small daily actions you take toward your goal, even if you don't see immediate results. Over time, these actions will compound

into larger achievements.

Example:

If your goal is to save more money, focus on the daily or weekly process of budgeting and making small savings contributions. Celebrate each successful week of sticking to your budget, rather than waiting until you've saved a significant amount to feel accomplished.

Tracking your progress and maintaining momentum are essential components of achieving long-term goals and building lasting habits. By using strategies like habit tracking, breaking goals into smaller milestones, reflecting on progress, implementing visual reminders, rewarding consistency, building accountability, and focusing on the process, you can create a system that keeps you motivated and moving forward.

These strategies help you celebrate each small victory, build momentum, and stay committed to your larger objectives. Ultimately, the key to success lies in consistency, perseverance, and finding ways to stay engaged with your progress every step of the way.

CHAPTER 5: OVERCOMING RESISTANCE: BREAKING BAD HABITS

*Why Bad Habits Are Difficult to Break and
How to Overcome Resistance*

Bad habits are behaviors that negatively affect our health, productivity, relationships, or overall well-being. Whether it's procrastination, overeating, smoking, or spending too much time on social media, we all have habits we'd like to change. Yet, breaking these bad habits can be incredibly difficult, even when we know they are harmful. Understanding why bad habits are hard to break and developing strategies to overcome this resistance are essential for achieving lasting change.

Why Bad Habits Are Difficult to Break

1. Habits Are Wired Into the Brain

Habits, both good and bad, are deeply ingrained in our brains. They form through a process called **habit loop**, which consists of three components: the **cue**, the **routine**, and the **reward**. Every time we engage in a habit, this loop is reinforced. Over time, the brain begins to automate the behavior, which means that the routine becomes an automatic response to the cue, and the reward further strengthens the habit.

For example, if you feel stressed (cue) and your routine is to reach for junk food (routine), the immediate pleasure (reward) reinforces this behavior. Because the brain prioritizes actions that lead to rewards, even if those rewards are short-lived, the habit becomes difficult to break.

2. Instant Gratification and Dopamine

One of the primary reasons bad habits are so difficult to break is the power of **instant gratification**. Bad habits often provide immediate rewards, even if the long-term consequences are negative. When you engage in a bad habit, such as eating unhealthy snacks or scrolling through social media, your brain releases **dopamine**, the "feel-good" neurotransmitter. This dopamine release creates a sense of pleasure, which reinforces the behavior and makes you more likely to repeat it in the future.

The challenge arises because our brains are hardwired to seek pleasure and avoid pain. Bad habits offer instant gratification, which feels rewarding in the short term, even if they harm us in the long run. This creates a cycle that is difficult to break.

3. **Routine and Familiarity**

Habits, whether good or bad, are often tied to routine and familiarity. Engaging in a bad habit might feel comfortable because it's what you're used to, even if you know it's not beneficial. Our brains are designed to conserve energy, which is why we default to behaviors that require minimal effort and decision-making. Bad habits are familiar, automatic responses that don't require much thought.

Breaking a bad habit, on the other hand, requires conscious effort and energy. It involves disrupting the habit loop, which can feel uncomfortable and exhausting. The resistance comes from our brain's natural inclination to stick with familiar patterns rather than embracing the discomfort of change.

4. **Emotional Triggers**

Many bad habits are driven by emotional triggers such as stress, boredom, loneliness, or anxiety. When we experience negative emotions, we often turn to our habits as coping mechanisms to soothe those feelings, even if the habit is detrimental in the long run. For example, stress might trigger someone to smoke a cigarette or eat unhealthy food because these behaviors provide temporary relief.

The emotional connection to bad habits makes them difficult

to break because the habit serves as a crutch for dealing with uncomfortable emotions. Until healthier coping mechanisms are developed, the bad habit will persist as a way to manage emotional stress.

How to Overcome Resistance and Break Bad Habits

Breaking bad habits is challenging, but it is possible with the right strategies and mindset. Below are some effective ways to overcome resistance and create lasting change.

1. **Identify the Cue-Reward Relationship**

To break a bad habit, you must first understand its components —the **cue** and **reward**. Identify what triggers the habit (cue) and what you gain from it (reward). For example, if you have a habit of checking your phone every time you're bored (cue) and the reward is a sense of distraction or temporary relief from boredom, you're more likely to repeat this behavior.

Once you understand the cue-reward relationship, you can begin to disrupt the habit loop by altering the routine. Instead of automatically reaching for your phone when you're bored, try substituting a different behavior that offers a similar reward, such as reading a book or going for a walk.

Actionable Tip: Keep a journal where you track the cue, routine, and reward of your bad habit. Over time, you'll begin to notice patterns and can experiment with changing the routine while keeping the same cue and reward.

2. **Start Small and Make Gradual Changes**

Trying to eliminate a bad habit all at once can be overwhelming and often leads to failure. Instead, start small by making gradual changes to the habit. For example, if you're trying to quit smoking, start by cutting down the number of cigarettes you smoke each day rather than quitting cold turkey. Small changes are easier to manage and lead to more sustainable success.

The key is to build positive momentum through small wins. As you start to make progress, your confidence will grow, and you'll be more motivated to continue making changes.

Actionable Tip: Break down the habit into smaller, more manageable steps. Set mini-goals for yourself, such as reducing your screen time by 10 minutes each day, and celebrate each small success.

3. Replace the Bad Habit with a Positive Habit

One of the most effective ways to break a bad habit is to **replace it with a positive habit**. Since habits are based on the cue-reward system, you don't need to eliminate the cue and reward; you just need to change the routine. For example, if stress triggers you to eat junk food, try replacing that behavior with a healthier coping mechanism, such as deep breathing exercises or a short walk.

By focusing on adding positive habits rather than just eliminating bad ones, you create a new routine that can deliver similar rewards in a healthier way.

Actionable Tip: Identify a positive habit that can serve as a replacement for your bad habit. For example, if you tend to procrastinate by watching TV, replace it with a quick productive task like decluttering a small space. Over time, this new habit will take the place of the old one.

4. Create a Plan for Managing Triggers

Since many bad habits are linked to emotional triggers, developing a plan for managing those triggers is essential. If stress, boredom, or anxiety tends to trigger your bad habits, find healthier ways to cope with those emotions. This might involve practicing mindfulness, engaging in hobbies, exercising, or talking to a friend.

Having a plan in place helps you anticipate when you're

likely to fall into old habits and provides you with alternative strategies to handle those situations.

Actionable Tip: Identify your emotional triggers and write down a list of healthy alternatives to manage them. For example, if stress triggers overeating, plan to take a five-minute break to practice deep breathing or call a friend for support instead of reaching for food.

5. Use Accountability and Support Systems

Breaking bad habits is easier when you have accountability and support. Whether it's a friend, family member, or coach, having someone to check in with you and offer encouragement can make a big difference. Accountability partners can help keep you on track, remind you of your goals, and celebrate your progress.

In addition to accountability, consider joining a support group or community of people who are also working to break similar habits. Sharing your journey with others can provide a sense of camaraderie and motivation.

Actionable Tip: Find an accountability partner or join a group that shares similar goals. Schedule regular check-ins to discuss your progress, challenges, and victories.

6. Practice Self-Compassion and Patience

Breaking bad habits takes time, and setbacks are a natural part of the process. It's important to practice self-compassion and be patient with yourself. Don't view setbacks as failures; instead, see them as opportunities to learn and grow.

Being kind to yourself during this process reduces the likelihood of giving up when things get difficult. Remember that lasting change doesn't happen overnight—it's a gradual process that requires consistency and perseverance.

Actionable Tip: If you experience a setback, take a moment to reflect on what led to the slip-up and how you can adjust your approach moving forward. Remind yourself that progress is not always linear and that every step forward counts.

Breaking bad habits is difficult because they are deeply ingrained in our brains, provide instant gratification, and often serve as coping mechanisms for emotional triggers. However, by understanding the mechanics of habit formation and applying strategic methods—such as identifying cues and rewards, making gradual changes, replacing bad habits with positive ones, managing emotional triggers, and seeking accountability—you can overcome resistance and create lasting change.

Remember that breaking bad habits is a journey, not a quick fix. By being patient, persistent, and compassionate with yourself, you can successfully overcome bad habits and replace them with healthier, more positive behaviors that support your long-term well-being and success.

Step-by-Step Guide to Identifying and Dismantling Harmful Habits

Harmful habits are behaviors that negatively impact your health, relationships, productivity, or overall well-being. While these habits can be difficult to break, they are not impossible to overcome. With a structured approach, you can identify and dismantle these habits, replacing them with more positive and productive behaviors. This guide provides a step-by-step approach to recognizing and eliminating harmful habits, so you can move toward healthier, more fulfilling choices.

Step 1: Identify the Harmful Habit

The first step in dismantling any harmful habit is to clearly identify what the habit is and recognize its impact on your life. Often, harmful habits can be subtle or ingrained in your routine, so it's important to take a close look at your behaviors and how they affect you.

Questions to Ask Yourself:

What behavior or habit do I consistently engage in that has negative consequences?
How does this habit impact my physical health, emotional well-being, relationships, or productivity?
When and where do I typically engage in this habit? Is it triggered by certain situations, people, or emotions?

Example: Suppose you've identified that mindless snacking throughout the day is a harmful habit. You've noticed that it leads to overeating, weight gain, and feelings of guilt. This habit might occur mostly when you're bored or stressed, and typically happens in the late afternoon or evening.

Action Step: Write down the habit you want to dismantle, along with the negative consequences it has on your life.

Step 2: Identify the Triggers (Cues)

Habits are often triggered by specific cues—situations, emotions, or environments that prompt you to engage in the behavior. The next step is to identify what triggers your harmful habit.

Questions to Ask Yourself:

What typically happens right before I engage in the habit? Is it a particular event, emotional state, or time of day?
Am I feeling a specific emotion (e.g., stress, boredom, loneliness) when this habit occurs?
Are there specific environments, people, or activities that encourage this habit?

Example: In the case of mindless snacking, you might realize that the habit is triggered by boredom or stress at work. Whenever you feel overwhelmed with a task or are trying to avoid work, you reach for a snack as a way to distract yourself or soothe your emotions.

Action Step: Track when and where the habit occurs over the course of a week. Write down the triggers you observe, such as time of day, emotions, or specific situations.

Step 3: Identify the Routine

The routine is the actual behavior that follows the cue. This is the habit itself—the action that you automatically perform in response to the trigger. To dismantle a harmful habit, it's essential to clearly define what this routine looks like.

Questions to Ask Yourself:

What behavior do I engage in after encountering the trigger?
How does this routine play out? Is it a short, quick behavior or something that takes longer?
Is this behavior something I do consciously, or does it feel automatic?

Example: After identifying boredom or stress as your trigger, you recognize that your routine is to go to the kitchen, grab a snack, and mindlessly eat while scrolling through social media or watching TV.

Action Step: Write down the specific routine you follow when the trigger occurs. This helps clarify the automatic nature of the habit and makes it easier to address.

Step 4: Identify the Reward

Every habit, even harmful ones, provides some form of reward, whether it's relief from stress, distraction from boredom, or a sense of comfort. Understanding what reward the habit provides is key to dismantling it because it helps you find alternative ways to achieve the same outcome.

Questions to Ask Yourself:

What positive feeling or relief do I experience after engaging in the habit?
Does this habit temporarily make me feel better, even if the long-term effects are negative?
What emotional or physical need is being met through this habit?

Example: You realize that the reward for your snacking habit is a sense of relief from stress or boredom. The snack provides a brief distraction and gives you a small burst of pleasure, even though the long-term result is guilt or discomfort.

Action Step: Write down the reward you receive from the habit. Be honest about the temporary positive feelings it provides, even if the habit is harmful overall.

Step 5: Find a Positive Substitute

Now that you've identified the trigger, routine, and reward, the next step is to find a positive substitute for the harmful habit. This substitute should offer the same reward but without the negative consequences. Replacing a harmful habit with a healthier one helps you maintain the cue-reward loop, but with a new, beneficial behavior.

Questions to Ask Yourself:

What alternative behavior can I engage in that provides a

similar reward but is healthier or more productive?
How can I incorporate this new behavior into my routine so that it becomes automatic?
Can I remove or reduce the cues that trigger the harmful habit?

Example: To replace mindless snacking, you might choose to take a five-minute walk whenever you feel bored or stressed. This new behavior provides relief from boredom and stress without the negative health consequences. Alternatively, you might choose to practice deep breathing exercises or have a glass of water instead of reaching for a snack.

Action Step: Choose a positive behavior to replace the harmful habit. Make sure it provides a similar reward and can be easily integrated into your routine.

Step 6: Plan for Obstacles and Challenges

Breaking a harmful habit is rarely a straightforward process. There will be obstacles and challenges along the way, such as moments of stress, temptation, or setbacks. Planning for these challenges in advance will help you stay on track and avoid reverting to the old habit.

Questions to Ask Yourself:

What situations or emotions might make it difficult to stick to my new habit?
How can I prepare for these challenges so that I don't fall back into old behaviors?
What will I do if I slip up and revert to the harmful habit?

Example: You anticipate that particularly stressful days at work will be challenging for sticking to your new habit of walking or deep breathing instead of snacking. To plan for this, you might keep a water bottle at your desk as a reminder to stay hydrated or schedule brief relaxation breaks to prevent stress from building up.

Action Step: Write down the potential challenges you might face and create a plan for dealing with them. This could include having reminders in place, finding an accountability partner, or adjusting your environment to reduce temptation.

Step 7: Track Your Progress and Celebrate Wins

Tracking your progress is essential for staying motivated and reinforcing your new habit. Celebrate small wins along the way, even if they seem insignificant. Positive reinforcement helps you stay committed and reminds you that change is possible, even if it's gradual.

Questions to Ask Yourself:

How can I track my progress to see the changes I'm making? What small victories can I celebrate to keep myself motivated? How will I reward myself for sticking to my new habit?

Example: You might use a habit tracker to mark each day that you successfully replace snacking with a healthier behavior. Each week, reward yourself with something enjoyable, like a relaxing activity or a small treat that aligns with your overall goals.

Action Step: Set up a system to track your progress, whether it's a journal, habit tracker, or app. Plan small rewards to celebrate your milestones and reinforce the positive change.

Step 8: Be Patient and Persistent

Breaking a harmful habit takes time and persistence. It's normal to experience setbacks or moments of temptation, but it's important to stay patient and committed to the process. Remember that changing habits is a gradual journey, not a quick fix.

Questions to Ask Yourself:

How can I stay patient and focused when progress feels slow?
What strategies will I use to stay motivated during challenging times?
How will I remind myself of the long-term benefits of breaking this habit?

Example: If you find yourself slipping back into mindless snacking, remind yourself that setbacks are a normal part of the process. Reflect on how much progress you've already made and recommit to your positive habit. Focus on the long-term benefits of improved health and well-being.

Action Step: Practice self-compassion and remind yourself that change is gradual. Stay focused on the progress you're making, no matter how small, and keep moving forward.

Dismantling harmful habits is a multi-step process that requires awareness, patience, and persistence. By identifying the triggers, routines, and rewards associated with your bad habits, and by replacing them with positive alternatives, you can create lasting change. Track your progress, celebrate small wins, and plan for obstacles so that you can maintain momentum and successfully break free from habits that no longer serve you. With consistent effort and a proactive approach, you can transform your behaviors and build a healthier, more fulfilling life.

Strategies for Breaking Bad Habits: Habit Substitution, Awareness Techniques, and Environmental Design

Breaking bad habits can be challenging, but certain strategies can make the process more manageable and effective. Three powerful approaches include **habit substitution, awareness techniques**, and **environmental design**. By applying these strategies, you can disrupt negative behavior patterns and create healthier, more sustainable habits.

1. Habit Substitution: Replacing Bad Habits with Positive Ones

Habit substitution is one of the most effective ways to break bad habits. The idea behind habit substitution is to replace the harmful behavior with a positive one that offers a similar reward. Since habits are driven by cues, routines, and rewards (known as the **habit loop**), you don't need to eliminate the loop altogether—just swap out the bad routine for a better one while keeping the same cue and reward.

How Habit Substitution Works

Identify the Cue: Determine what triggers your bad habit. This could be an emotional state (e.g., stress), a specific time of day (e.g., after lunch), or a particular environment (e.g., being around certain people).

Replace the Routine: Once you've identified the cue, focus on changing the routine. The key is to find a positive behavior that fulfills the same need as the bad habit but in a healthier or more productive way.

Maintain the Reward: The new behavior should provide a reward similar to the one you got from the bad habit. This could be a sense of relaxation, pleasure, or accomplishment.

Example of Habit Substitution

Bad Habit: Stress-eating unhealthy snacks in the afternoon.
Cue: Feeling stressed or overwhelmed at work.
Routine: Eating sugary snacks to cope with stress.
Reward: Temporary relief and a boost in energy.

To substitute this habit, you could replace the routine of stress-eating with a healthier alternative:

New Routine: Practice deep breathing exercises or take a short walk whenever you feel stressed.
Reward: You still get the relief from stress but in a way that supports your overall well-being.

By consistently practicing the new behavior, the bad habit of stress-eating can be gradually replaced by a more beneficial habit like mindfulness or physical activity.

Tips for Habit Substitution

Start Small: Make the new habit simple and easy to implement, especially in the beginning.
Be Consistent: The more often you practice the new routine in response to the cue, the quicker it will become ingrained.
Use Habit Stacking: Attach the new habit to an existing habit. For example, if you want to replace mindless phone scrolling before bed, you might substitute it with a five-minute gratitude journaling session right after brushing your teeth.

2. Awareness Techniques: Increasing Consciousness of Your Habits

Many habits, especially bad ones, operate on autopilot. **Awareness techniques** are strategies designed to increase your consciousness of these behaviors, making it easier to identify and interrupt harmful patterns.

How Awareness Techniques Work

Awareness techniques help you tune into your habits as they happen, giving you a chance to pause and reflect before engaging in the behavior. By becoming more mindful of your actions, you can create the mental space needed to choose a different response.

Examples of Awareness Techniques

1. **Mindfulness and Meditation**

Mindfulness meditation helps you cultivate awareness of your thoughts, feelings, and behaviors. By regularly practicing mindfulness, you become more attuned to the triggers that lead to your bad habits. This increased awareness allows you to catch yourself in the moment and make a conscious decision to choose a different behavior.

Example: If you tend to reach for your phone every time you feel bored, practicing mindfulness can help you notice the urge as it arises. Instead of automatically picking up your phone, you might choose to engage in a mindful activity like taking a few deep breaths or practicing a short meditation.

2. **Journaling and Habit Tracking**

Journaling can help you identify patterns in your behavior and emotions that contribute to your habits. By writing down when, where, and why you engage in a bad habit, you can uncover triggers and emotional states that you may not have been aware of.

Example: If you have a habit of procrastinating on important tasks, keeping a journal of your daily activities and emotional states can help you pinpoint the specific triggers (e.g., anxiety about the task) that cause you to delay. With this awareness, you can then focus on addressing the underlying emotions rather than avoiding the task.

3. **Trigger Journaling**

This technique involves actively recording every time you experience a cue that leads to a bad habit. By keeping a log of these moments, you increase your awareness of the situations, thoughts, and feelings that trigger the habit. This awareness can help you anticipate and manage the triggers before the habit takes over.

Example: If you're trying to quit smoking, carry a small notebook with you and jot down each time you feel the urge to smoke. Include details such as where you are, who you're with, and what you're feeling. Over time, you'll notice patterns and can take steps to avoid or address these triggers.

Tips for Awareness Techniques

Be Consistent: Practice mindfulness or journaling regularly to develop a deeper awareness of your habits.
Create Reminders: Set alarms or use sticky notes as reminders to check in with yourself throughout the day. These prompts help bring your awareness back to the present moment.
Focus on Reflection: After journaling or practicing mindfulness, reflect on what you've noticed about your habits and use that information to guide your behavior change.

3. Environmental Design: Structuring Your Environment for Success

Your environment plays a significant role in shaping your habits. **Environmental design** is the practice of arranging your surroundings to make good habits easier to perform and bad habits harder to engage in. By modifying your environment, you can reduce temptation and create cues that support your desired behaviors.

How Environmental Design Works

The principle behind environmental design is simple: make good habits the path of least resistance and bad habits more difficult to execute. Small changes in your surroundings can have a profound impact on your behavior.

Examples of Environmental Design

1. **Remove Triggers and Temptations**

One of the easiest ways to break a bad habit is to remove the things that trigger it from your environment. By eliminating or reducing exposure to these triggers, you reduce the likelihood of engaging in the habit.

Example: If you're trying to cut down on junk food, remove unhealthy snacks from your home and replace them with healthier options like fruit or nuts. This makes it more difficult to engage in the bad habit of unhealthy snacking, while making it easier to choose healthier alternatives.

2. **Create Positive Cues**

Design your environment to cue positive behaviors. For example, if you want to build a habit of exercising in the morning, lay out your workout clothes the night before so they're the first thing you see when you wake up.

Example: If you're trying to drink more water, place a water bottle in visible locations around your home and office. The visual cue will remind you to hydrate throughout the day.

3. **Change Your Physical Environment**

Sometimes, breaking a habit requires changing the physical space where the habit occurs. If your bad habit is tied to a specific location or routine, changing your environment can help disrupt the behavior.

Example: If you find yourself constantly distracted while working from home, create a dedicated workspace that is free from distractions like the TV or your phone. Rearranging your environment in this way can help you focus and reduce the temptation to engage in unproductive habits.

Breaking bad habits requires a combination of strategies that address the behavioral, emotional, and environmental factors that sustain those habits. **Habit substitution**, **awareness techniques**, and **environmental design** are three powerful approaches that can help you dismantle harmful behaviors and replace them with positive ones. By identifying the triggers and rewards of your habits, increasing your awareness of automatic behaviors, and structuring your environment for success, you create the conditions needed to support long-term change.

With consistent effort and strategic planning, you can break free from bad habits and build a healthier, more fulfilling life.

CHAPTER 6: BUILDING RESILIENCE: STICKING TO YOUR NEW HABITS

The Importance of Resilience When Habits Are Disrupted

In the journey of habit formation, setbacks and failures are inevitable. Life is unpredictable, and even the most well-established habits can be disrupted by unexpected events, such as illness, work stress, family emergencies, or a simple loss of motivation. This is where **resilience** becomes a critical factor in maintaining long-term success. Resilience, in this context, refers to your ability to recover quickly from setbacks, adapt to challenges, and continue working toward your goals despite obstacles. It is the trait that allows you to keep going, even when your habits are disrupted.

Understanding the importance of resilience, learning how to cultivate it, and knowing how to respond to disruptions are key to staying on track with your habits and achieving long-term success. This article explores why resilience is essential in habit formation, the challenges you may face, and strategies to build and maintain resilience when your habits are disrupted.

Why Resilience Is Critical for Habit Formation

1. Setbacks Are Inevitable

When trying to build new habits or sustain existing ones, setbacks are part of the process. No one maintains perfect consistency 100% of the time. You may miss a workout, fall back into old eating patterns, skip your daily meditation, or procrastinate on work tasks. These disruptions can be caused by external factors (such as a busy schedule or unforeseen circumstances) or internal factors (like stress, exhaustion, or a lack of motivation).

Without resilience, these setbacks can lead to frustration, self-doubt, and the temptation to abandon your efforts altogether. However, with resilience, you're able to see setbacks as temporary and part of the journey rather than as signs of failure.

2. Habits Take Time to Solidify

Research shows that it can take anywhere from 21 to 66 days —or longer—for a habit to become automatic. During this time, you are particularly vulnerable to disruptions. The early stages of habit formation require consistency, but they also demand flexibility. Resilience helps you stay committed to the process, even when progress feels slow or when you encounter obstacles.

By developing resilience, you learn to accept that habit formation is not linear. You might make progress for several days or weeks, only to experience a setback. Instead of giving up, resilience allows you to bounce back, adjust your approach, and keep moving forward.

3. Resilience Encourages Growth

Setbacks provide valuable learning opportunities. They force you to assess what went wrong, why you encountered difficulties, and how you can adapt your habits to fit changing circumstances. Resilience fosters a **growth mindset**—the belief that challenges are opportunities for growth rather than signs of failure.

For example, if a demanding work schedule prevents you from maintaining your workout routine, resilience encourages you to reflect on the situation and find alternative solutions. You might adjust your workout schedule, shorten your exercise sessions, or incorporate more movement into your daily routine. This process of adapting to challenges strengthens both your habits and your ability to persevere through adversity.

The Challenges of Maintaining Habits During Disruptions

Several challenges can arise when your habits are disrupted. Understanding these challenges is the first step to overcoming them with resilience.

1. Perfectionism

One of the biggest challenges in habit formation is the desire for perfection. Many people approach new habits with an "all-or-nothing" mindset, believing that any deviation from their plan is a sign of failure. This mindset can make it difficult to recover from setbacks because even small disruptions feel like insurmountable failures.

2. Loss of Motivation

Motivation naturally fluctuates over time. When habits are disrupted, especially during stressful periods, your motivation to continue can wane. This can lead to a downward spiral where you feel discouraged by your lack of progress, which in turn reduces your motivation to start again.

3. Self-Criticism

When you experience setbacks, it's common to engage in self-criticism. You might blame yourself for not being disciplined enough, feel guilty about your lack of consistency, or label yourself as a failure. This self-criticism can further erode your motivation and make it harder to recover from disruptions.

Strategies for Building Resilience When Habits Are Disrupted

Resilience is not an inherent trait; it's a skill that can be developed and strengthened over time. Below are strategies to build resilience and maintain momentum when your habits are disrupted.

1. Adopt a Growth Mindset

A growth mindset is the belief that challenges, setbacks, and failures are opportunities for growth rather than indicators of personal inadequacy. When you adopt a growth mindset, you understand that disruptions are part of the learning process. Instead of viewing them as failures, you see them as opportunities to refine your habits and become more adaptable.

Actionable Tip: After a setback, ask yourself: "What can I learn from this?" Reflect on what triggered the disruption and how you can adjust your habits or environment to prevent it from happening again.

2. Practice Self-Compassion

Self-compassion is crucial when dealing with setbacks. Instead of engaging in negative self-talk or blaming yourself for not being perfect, practice kindness and understanding toward yourself. Recognize that everyone faces challenges and that progress is more important than perfection.

Actionable Tip: Treat yourself as you would treat a friend who is struggling. If a friend came to you feeling discouraged after a setback, you would likely offer support and encouragement. Offer that same compassion to yourself.

3. Focus on Consistency, Not Perfection

Perfection is unattainable, but consistency is key to habit formation. Focus on showing up regularly, even if you can't follow your habit perfectly every time. If you miss a day, don't let it derail your progress. Instead, recommit to your habit the next day.

Actionable Tip: Use the "never miss twice" rule. If you miss one day of your habit, make sure to get back on track the next day.

This approach helps prevent small setbacks from turning into long-term disruptions.

4. Redefine Success

Redefine what success looks like during times of disruption. If you're going through a particularly busy or stressful period, success might look different than it does when things are going smoothly. Adjust your expectations and celebrate small victories, even if they don't match your original plan.

Actionable Tip: Set smaller, more achievable goals during times of disruption. For example, if you're struggling to maintain your usual 30-minute workout routine, aim for 10 minutes of movement instead. This keeps the habit alive while accommodating your current circumstances.

5. Create Flexible Habits

Rigid habits are more susceptible to disruption. Instead, design your habits to be flexible enough to adapt to changes in your schedule or energy levels. This flexibility allows you to maintain your habits even when life throws you a curveball.

Actionable Tip: Create different versions of your habit based on your circumstances. For example, you might have a "high-energy" version of your habit (a 30-minute workout) and a "low-energy" version (a 10-minute walk). This way, you can adjust your habit based on how you're feeling or what your day looks like.

6. Reframe Setbacks as Temporary

One of the most important aspects of resilience is the ability to see setbacks as temporary. Instead of viewing disruptions as the end of your habit, remind yourself that they are just a pause. By reframing setbacks in this way, you prevent them from derailing your long-term progress.

Actionable Tip: When you experience a setback, tell yourself,

"This is just a temporary pause, not a failure." This mindset shift helps you maintain perspective and reduces the emotional impact of the disruption.

7. Develop a Plan for Getting Back on Track

Having a plan for how you will get back on track after a setback is essential. This plan should be simple and actionable, focusing on small steps that help you regain momentum. By knowing exactly what you'll do to recover from a disruption, you reduce the likelihood of letting setbacks snowball into long-term lapses.

Actionable Tip: Create a "recovery plan" for your habits. For example, if you miss a few days of your meditation practice, your recovery plan might include setting aside 5 minutes the next morning to meditate, regardless of what else is happening that day. Keep the plan simple and actionable to ensure you can implement it easily.

Resilience is the key to maintaining momentum when your habits are disrupted. By adopting a growth mindset, practicing self-compassion, focusing on consistency rather than perfection, and creating flexible habits, you can navigate setbacks and continue moving toward your goals. Setbacks are a natural part of the habit formation process, but they don't have to derail your progress. With resilience, you can recover from disruptions, learn from challenges, and build habits that stand the test of time.

Remember, the journey of habit formation is not about achieving perfection but about showing up consistently and adapting to the inevitable ups and downs along the way. By building resilience, you empower yourself to keep going, even when the path gets difficult.

Strategies for Maintaining Habits During Stressful Times or

Life Transitions

Stressful times and major life transitions—such as starting a new job, moving to a new city, or experiencing personal challenges—can disrupt even the most well-established habits. During these periods, it can be easy to let go of your routines, but maintaining healthy habits is essential for both your physical and mental well-being. While it's natural for habits to be affected during times of stress, there are strategies you can employ to ensure they remain a stable part of your life. In this article, we'll explore practical ways to maintain your habits during stressful times or life transitions.

1. Set Realistic Expectations and Adapt Your Habits

When life gets stressful, trying to maintain your habits at the same level of intensity can be overwhelming and lead to burnout. Instead of expecting to continue at full capacity, **adapt your habits** to fit your current situation. Lowering the bar temporarily is not a failure—it's a smart way to ensure that you remain consistent during challenging periods.

How to Adapt Your Habits:

Scale Down: If you're used to exercising for 45 minutes a day but find that impossible during a stressful time, scale it down to 10 or 15 minutes. The key is to keep the habit alive, even in a smaller form.

Create a Minimum Viable Habit: Develop a "bare minimum" version of your habit that you can do even on your busiest or most stressful days. For example, if you usually meditate for 20 minutes, your minimum viable habit might be meditating for just 5 minutes.

Be Flexible: Life transitions often require adjustments to your schedule, so be open to modifying the timing of your habits. If your usual morning routine is disrupted, find another time during the day to practice your habit, even if it's not at the ideal moment.

Example: If you're experiencing a lot of stress at work and can't stick to your full exercise routine, switch to a 10-minute daily walk. It keeps you active and reinforces the habit, even in a reduced form.

2. Focus on Keystone Habits

Keystone habits are those that have a positive ripple effect on other areas of your life. By focusing on maintaining these core habits, you can ensure that you continue to see benefits, even when other routines may fall by the wayside. Keystone habits often serve as a foundation for other positive behaviors, so keeping them intact can help you stay grounded during times of stress.

How to Identify Keystone Habits:

- **Prioritize What Matters Most**: Think about which habits have the most significant impact on your well-being and productivity. Common keystone habits include exercise, sleep, meditation, healthy eating, and planning your day.
- **Maintain Simplicity**: Focus on one or two keystone habits that are non-negotiable. These habits should be relatively simple to maintain but offer significant returns in terms of energy, focus, and stress management.

Example: If exercise is your keystone habit, prioritize maintaining it, even if other habits are disrupted. A short daily workout or walk might help you manage stress, improve your mood, and encourage healthier eating and sleep habits.

3. Plan for Disruptions

Expecting life to continue as usual during stressful times is unrealistic. Instead, anticipate disruptions and plan for them in advance. Having a plan allows you to respond proactively when your routine is thrown off track, rather than letting stress or transition completely derail your habits.

How to Plan for Disruptions:

Identify Potential Challenges: Reflect on what kinds of disruptions are most likely to affect your habits during stressful times. For example, will work deadlines keep you from exercising, or will travel interfere with your meal planning?
Create Contingency Plans: Develop strategies for maintaining your habits when disruptions occur. This might include adjusting your schedule, setting up reminders, or finding alternative ways to practice your habits.
Be Flexible with Your Plan: Understand that your plan may need to evolve as circumstances change. Allow yourself the flexibility to adjust as needed.

Example: If you anticipate that a busy work week will disrupt your usual gym routine, plan to do shorter home workouts instead. This way, you're prepared to maintain the habit even when your schedule changes.

4. Simplify and Prioritize Self-Care

During stressful periods, it's easy to become overwhelmed by the demands of life and let self-care habits slip. However, self-care is especially important when you're under stress. **Simplify your self-care habits** to make them more manageable during tough times.

How to Simplify and Prioritize Self-Care:

Identify Core Self-Care Needs: Determine the self-care habits that are most crucial for your well-being, such as sleep, hydration, nutrition, and relaxation.
Simplify Your Routine: Focus on the simplest and most effective self-care practices. For example, prioritize getting enough sleep or taking regular breaks, even if other habits take a back seat.
Schedule Time for Self-Care: Build small self-care practices into your schedule, even if it's just a few minutes a day. During

times of stress, intentionally carving out time for self-care is essential.

Example: If you're going through a stressful period, prioritize getting 7-8 hours of sleep each night and drinking plenty of water throughout the day. These simple self-care practices can help you manage stress and maintain your energy levels.

5. Leverage Support Systems and Accountability

During times of stress or transition, it's easy to feel isolated or overwhelmed. Leveraging your **support system**—whether it's friends, family, or an accountability partner—can help you stay on track with your habits. Having someone to check in with or lean on can provide motivation, encouragement, and accountability.

How to Leverage Support Systems:

Find an Accountability Partner: Choose someone who shares similar goals or habits and check in with each other regularly. This could be a friend, coworker, or family member who helps you stay committed to your habits.

Join a Community or Group: Communities, whether online or in-person, can provide collective support during stressful times. For example, if you're trying to maintain a fitness habit, joining an online workout community can help keep you motivated.

Ask for Help: Don't hesitate to ask for help from your support network when you're feeling overwhelmed. Whether it's asking a friend to help you with meal prep or taking a walk together, small acts of support can help you maintain your habits.

Example: If you're struggling to stick to your habits during a life transition, ask a friend to check in with you regularly about your progress. Knowing someone else is holding you accountable can help keep you on track.

6. Practice Self-Compassion and Adjust Expectations

One of the most important things you can do during stressful times is to practice self-compassion. Life transitions and periods of stress are hard, and it's normal for your habits to be affected. Instead of criticizing yourself for not being perfect, give yourself grace and adjust your expectations.

How to Practice Self-Compassion:

Accept that you may not be able to maintain your habits perfectly during stressful times, and that's okay. Focus on doing your best, even if it's less than what you normally expect from yourself.

Acknowledge and celebrate the small victories, even if they seem insignificant. This helps reinforce your efforts and keeps you motivated.

When setbacks occur, respond with kindness rather than self-criticism. Remind yourself that setbacks are temporary, and that you can always get back on track.

Example: If you miss a few days of your habit due to a life transition, don't beat yourself up. Instead, acknowledge that it's a challenging time and celebrate the fact that you're still committed to maintaining your habits, even if they're not perfect.

7. Incorporate Mindfulness and Stress-Relief Techniques

Mindfulness and stress-relief techniques can help you stay grounded during stressful times, making it easier to maintain your habits. These practices help you manage the emotional and physical effects of stress, allowing you to stay focused and centered.

How to Incorporate Mindfulness and Stress Relief:

Practice mindful breathing for a few minutes each day to help reduce stress and anxiety. This can be done anywhere, at any time, making it an easy habit to maintain.

Write down a few things you're grateful for each day. Focusing on gratitude helps shift your mindset from stress to positivity, making it easier to stay motivated.

If meditation is part of your routine, try shorter, more frequent sessions during stressful times. Even five minutes of meditation can help calm your mind and reduce stress.

Example: During a particularly stressful time, commit to practicing mindful breathing for five minutes every morning. This simple practice helps you stay centered and reduces the emotional impact of stress, making it easier to stick to your other habits.

Maintaining habits during stressful times or life transitions is challenging, but it's not impossible. By setting realistic expectations, focusing on keystone habits, planning for disruptions, simplifying your routines, leveraging support systems, practicing self-compassion, and incorporating mindfulness techniques, you can keep your habits alive even in difficult circumstances. Remember, the key is not perfection but consistency. By making small adjustments and remaining flexible, you can maintain your habits and continue to grow, even when life feels overwhelming.

Introducing the Concept of "Habit Stacking" for Reinforcing New Routines

Building new habits can be challenging, especially when you're trying to integrate them into an already busy schedule. One powerful and effective method for making new habits stick is called **habit stacking**. Habit stacking is a simple, yet transformative, technique that involves pairing a new habit with an existing habit that's already ingrained in your daily routine. By connecting the new habit to a well-established one, you create a mental cue, making it easier for the new behavior to become automatic and consistent.

In this article, we will explore the concept of habit stacking, why it works, how to implement it, and how it can help reinforce new routines in your life.

What Is Habit Stacking?

Habit stacking, a term popularized by James Clear in his book *Atomic Habits*, is based on the idea of anchoring a new habit to an existing habit. The theory behind habit stacking draws on the science of habit loops—cue, routine, and reward—where a cue triggers a behavior, and the behavior provides a reward. By using a habit that you already perform consistently as the cue for a new habit, you make it easier for the new behavior to take root.

For example, if you already have the habit of brushing your teeth every morning, you could use this established routine as the cue to trigger a new habit, such as flossing or practicing gratitude. Over time, the new behavior will become linked to the existing habit, making it easier to perform without conscious effort.

Why Habit Stacking Works

Habit stacking works because it leverages the power of **association**. Rather than trying to remember to do a new habit on its own, you anchor it to something you're already doing regularly. This creates a mental link between the two behaviors, allowing the established habit to serve as a trigger for the new one.

Key Reasons Habit Stacking Is Effective:

1. **Takes Advantage of Existing Routines**: You're not starting from scratch. By building on something you

already do, the process feels more natural and less daunting.
2. **Provides a Clear Cue**: The existing habit serves as a clear and consistent cue for the new behavior, reducing the need for reminders or excessive willpower.
3. **Simplifies Habit Formation**: Habit stacking makes new behaviors easier to remember and implement, which increases the likelihood of long-term success.
4. **Builds Consistency**: Since the existing habit is already part of your routine, the new habit benefits from the same regularity, helping it to become consistent more quickly.

How to Implement Habit Stacking

Habit stacking is a straightforward technique, but it requires thoughtful planning to execute effectively. Here are the steps to successfully implement habit stacking and reinforce new routines.

Step 1: Identify a Current Habit

The first step in habit stacking is to identify a current habit that is already firmly established in your daily routine. This habit should be something you do automatically and without much thought—such as brushing your teeth, making coffee, or locking the door when you leave the house.

Questions to Ask Yourself:

What are some habits I do consistently every day, without fail? Are there daily tasks I perform automatically, such as getting dressed or checking my email?

Examples of Current Habits:

Brushing your teeth
Drinking your morning coffee
Taking a shower

Eating breakfast
Arriving at work

Once you've identified a solid, existing habit, you'll use it as the foundation for stacking a new behavior.

Step 2: Choose a New Habit

Next, decide on a new habit you want to incorporate into your routine. This could be anything related to your goals, such as drinking more water, practicing mindfulness, stretching, or reading. The key is to select a habit that is small, manageable, and something you can easily attach to your existing routine.

Questions to Ask Yourself:

What new habit do I want to establish?
How can I make this habit simple and actionable, so it's easy to start?

Examples of New Habits:

Meditating for 2 minutes
Writing down 3 things you're grateful for
Flossing your teeth
Drinking a glass of water
Doing 10 pushups or a quick stretch

Step 3: Pair the New Habit with the Existing Habit

The next step is to pair the new habit with your existing habit. This is the essence of habit stacking—linking the new behavior to the old one so that it becomes part of the same routine. Think of your existing habit as the "cue" and the new habit as the "response."

Formula for Habit Stacking: After/Before [current habit], I will [new habit].

This formula helps you clearly define when and where the new habit will occur. By tying the new habit to something already established, you create a seamless transition between the two actions.

Examples of Habit Stacking:

After I brush my teeth in the morning, I will floss.
Before I drink my morning coffee, I will write down three things I am grateful for.
After I sit down at my desk at work, I will drink a glass of water.
Before I turn off my phone for the night, I will meditate for 5 minutes.

Step 4: Start Small and Build Gradually

When starting with habit stacking, it's important to begin with small, easily achievable habits. The new behavior should take minimal effort and be realistic to implement. Starting small makes it easier to stay consistent, which is essential for the habit to stick.

As the new habit becomes more automatic, you can gradually increase the intensity or duration. For example, once you've consistently meditated for 2 minutes, you can extend it to 5 or 10 minutes.

Tips for Starting Small:

Focus on micro-habits that take less than two minutes to complete.
Don't overwhelm yourself by trying to stack multiple habits at once. Start with one habit stack, and once it's solid, you can add more.

Step 5: Track Your Progress and Adjust as Needed

Tracking your progress is a valuable way to reinforce your habit stacking efforts. Keep a simple habit tracker or journal to record when you successfully complete your new habit. Seeing your progress helps build momentum and keeps you motivated.

In addition, pay attention to how the habit stack feels over time. If the new habit isn't sticking, reassess the pairing. Maybe the existing habit isn't the best cue, or the new habit needs to be simplified further. Habit stacking is flexible, so don't be afraid to adjust as needed.

Ways to Track Progress:

Use a habit-tracking app or a simple checklist to mark each day you complete the habit stack.
Reflect weekly on how well the habit stack is working and if any adjustments are needed.

Step 6: Celebrate Your Successes

Each time you successfully complete your habit stack, take a moment to celebrate. Positive reinforcement is key to making habits stick, and even small celebrations can help reinforce the behavior.

Celebrating your success doesn't have to be elaborate. It could be as simple as giving yourself a mental high-five, checking off the habit on your tracker, or rewarding yourself with something enjoyable after completing the habit.

Habit Stacking Examples in Everyday Life

Here are a few examples of how habit stacking can be applied to different areas of life:

1. Morning Routine

After I pour my morning coffee, I will read one page of a book.
After I get dressed for the day, I will do 5 minutes of stretching.

2. Workday Routine

Before I open my laptop at work, I will review my top three priorities for the day.
After I finish a meeting, I will take a 2-minute walk to clear my head.

3. Evening Routine

After I set my alarm for the next day, I will practice 3 minutes of deep breathing.
After I eat dinner, I will clean the kitchen for 10 minutes.

Habit stacking is a powerful technique for building new habits by connecting them to existing routines. By taking advantage of habits you already perform automatically, you can establish new behaviors with less effort and more consistency. Whether you're looking to improve your health, productivity, or personal growth, habit stacking allows you to seamlessly integrate new habits into your daily life. The simplicity and effectiveness of habit stacking lie in its ability to create clear cues and make new behaviors feel natural and effortless. Start by identifying one existing habit and pair it with a small, actionable new habit. Over time, you'll find that habit stacking helps you build routines that support your long-term goals and personal development.

CHAPTER 7: HABITS IN HEALTH AND WELLNESS

The Importance of Health-Related Habits: Exercise, Nutrition, and Sleep

Health-related habits, such as regular exercise, proper nutrition, and adequate sleep, form the foundation of our physical and mental well-being. These habits not only impact how we feel on a day-to-day basis but also contribute to our long-term health, energy levels, emotional balance, and even productivity. Developing and maintaining these habits is essential for living a healthier, happier, and more fulfilled life. This article explores the importance of health-related habits and provides insights into why they are crucial for overall well-being.

1. The Role of Exercise in Health

Regular exercise is one of the most important habits you can cultivate for your physical and mental health. Exercise offers numerous benefits, ranging from improved cardiovascular health to enhanced mood and cognitive function. Whether you engage in intense workouts, yoga, or simple daily walks, consistent physical activity can transform your health.

Key Benefits of Exercise:

Physical Health: Regular exercise strengthens your heart, improves circulation, and reduces the risk of chronic diseases like heart disease, diabetes, and obesity. It also helps build and maintain muscle strength, flexibility, and endurance.

Mental Health: Exercise has been shown to reduce symptoms of anxiety and depression by triggering the release of endorphins —natural chemicals in the brain that improve mood and reduce stress. Physical activity also promotes better sleep and boosts self-esteem.

Cognitive Function: Exercise improves brain health by increasing blood flow to the brain, promoting the growth of new neurons, and enhancing cognitive function. Regular physical activity has been linked to improved memory, sharper focus, and better problem-solving skills.

Longevity: Studies consistently show that individuals who engage in regular exercise tend to live longer, healthier lives. Physical activity helps protect against age-related declines in muscle mass, mobility, and cognitive function, allowing you to maintain a high quality of life as you age.

How to Build an Exercise Habit:

Building an exercise habit requires consistency and a realistic approach. Start small and gradually increase the intensity or duration of your workouts. Choose activities you enjoy, whether it's dancing, cycling, hiking, or lifting weights, to make the habit more sustainable. Integrating exercise into your daily routine—like walking during lunch breaks or doing bodyweight exercises at home—can help you stay active even when your schedule is busy.

2. The Importance of Proper Nutrition

Good nutrition is another fundamental health-related habit that plays a critical role in your overall well-being. The food you eat provides the nutrients your body needs to function optimally, impacting everything from your energy levels to your immune system and mental clarity.

Key Benefits of Proper Nutrition:

Energy Levels: Proper nutrition fuels your body with the energy it needs to carry out daily activities. A diet rich in whole foods —such as fruits, vegetables, whole grains, lean proteins, and healthy fats—provides sustained energy and helps prevent the energy crashes that often come with processed or sugary foods.

Weight Management: A balanced diet helps regulate body weight by providing the right amount of calories and nutrients. It also promotes a healthy metabolism and supports the maintenance of muscle mass, both of which are important for weight management.

Disease Prevention: Good nutrition helps reduce the risk of chronic diseases such as heart disease, diabetes, and certain cancers. Diets rich in antioxidants, fiber, and essential vitamins and minerals help protect the body from inflammation and oxidative stress, which are major contributors to disease.

Immune Function: Nutrients like vitamins A, C, and E, as well as zinc and selenium, are vital for maintaining a strong immune system. A diet rich in fruits and vegetables provides these nutrients, helping to protect the body from infections and illnesses.

Mental Health: What you eat also affects your brain health. Diets high in processed foods and sugar are linked to an increased risk of depression and anxiety, while nutrient-dense diets—particularly those rich in omega-3 fatty acids, vitamins, and minerals—can support better mental health and cognitive function.

How to Build a Nutrition Habit:

Building healthy eating habits starts with small, consistent changes. Focus on incorporating more whole foods into your diet, such as vegetables, fruits, lean proteins, and whole grains, while gradually reducing your intake of processed foods, sugary snacks, and excessive amounts of unhealthy fats. Meal planning, portion control, and mindful eating practices can help you develop a more balanced approach to nutrition.

3. The Necessity of Adequate Sleep

Sleep is often an overlooked aspect of health, but it is just as important as exercise and nutrition for your overall well-being.

Adequate sleep is essential for physical recovery, cognitive function, emotional regulation, and immune system health.

Key Benefits of Sleep:

Physical Recovery: During sleep, your body repairs and regenerates tissues, builds muscle, and strengthens the immune system. Without sufficient sleep, these processes are impaired, leading to increased vulnerability to illness, slower recovery from exercise, and a higher risk of injury.

Cognitive Function: Sleep is crucial for brain health and cognitive function. It allows the brain to consolidate memories, process information, and clear out toxins that accumulate during wakefulness. A lack of sleep can lead to impaired decision-making, difficulty concentrating, and memory problems.

Emotional Regulation: Sleep has a significant impact on your emotional health. Sleep deprivation can make it harder to regulate emotions, leading to irritability, mood swings, and an increased risk of anxiety and depression. Adequate sleep helps maintain emotional balance and resilience.

Metabolic Health: Sleep plays a key role in regulating hormones that control appetite and metabolism. Insufficient sleep can disrupt these hormones, leading to increased hunger, cravings for unhealthy foods, and a higher risk of weight gain and obesity.

Immune Function: During sleep, your body produces cytokines —proteins that help fight infection, inflammation, and stress. Sleep deprivation weakens the immune system, making you more susceptible to illnesses like the common cold and flu.

How to Build a Sleep Habit:

To improve your sleep habits, prioritize creating a consistent sleep schedule by going to bed and waking up at the same time every day, even on weekends. Establish a relaxing bedtime routine, such as reading, meditating, or taking a warm bath, to signal to your body that it's time to wind down. Limit screen time and exposure to blue light before bed, as these can interfere with the production of melatonin, the hormone that regulates sleep. Aim for 7-9 hours of sleep per night, depending on your individual needs.

The Interconnectedness of Exercise, Nutrition, and Sleep

One of the most important things to understand about exercise, nutrition, and sleep is that they are **interconnected**. Each habit affects the others, creating a positive feedback loop when maintained consistently.

Exercise and Sleep: Regular exercise can improve sleep quality by helping you fall asleep faster and stay asleep longer. Additionally, better sleep leads to improved exercise performance, enhancing physical recovery and endurance.
Nutrition and Sleep: Proper nutrition supports better sleep by stabilizing blood sugar levels and providing the body with the nutrients needed for restorative rest. In turn, sufficient sleep helps regulate hunger hormones, reducing cravings for unhealthy foods.
Exercise and Nutrition: Regular exercise supports healthy eating habits by boosting metabolism and encouraging mindful eating. When you're physically active, you're more likely to make food choices that align with your fitness goals, such as choosing nutrient-dense meals that fuel your workouts and aid recovery.

By focusing on all three habits—exercise, nutrition, and sleep—you create a solid foundation for overall health and well-being. Each habit reinforces the others, leading to improved energy levels, better mental clarity, enhanced emotional resilience, and a stronger immune system.

Health-related habits, such as regular exercise, proper nutrition, and adequate sleep, are essential for achieving and maintaining a healthy, balanced lifestyle. These habits provide a wide range of physical, mental, and emotional benefits, from reducing the risk of chronic disease to improving mood and cognitive function.

Building and sustaining these habits requires consistency, flexibility, and a commitment to self-care. By incorporating small, manageable changes into your daily routine, you can create lasting health habits that enhance your overall quality of life. When exercise, nutrition, and sleep work together, they create a positive cycle that promotes long-term well-being, resilience, and vitality.

Actionable Tips for Developing Habits that Promote Physical and Mental Well-Being

Building habits that support physical and mental well-being is one of the most effective ways to improve your overall quality of life. By incorporating consistent, healthy behaviors into your daily routine, you can boost your energy, reduce stress, enhance your mood, and improve your overall health. Here are some actionable tips for developing habits that promote both physical and mental well-being.

1. Start Small and Be Consistent

The key to building sustainable habits is to **start small** and focus on consistency over perfection. Trying to overhaul your life all at once is often overwhelming and unsustainable. Instead, choose one or two small habits to focus on and gradually build from there.

Tip: Begin with micro-habits that are easy to implement. For example, if you want to build an exercise habit, start with just 5 minutes of movement per day. Once that becomes routine, you can gradually increase the duration or intensity.
Example: If you want to meditate, begin with 2 minutes of deep breathing in the morning. Once this becomes a natural part of

your day, you can expand to longer meditation sessions.

2. Create a Morning Routine for Mental Clarity

How you start your day can set the tone for the rest of it. Developing a **morning routine** that supports your mental well-being can help you feel grounded, focused, and prepared for whatever the day brings.

Tip: Include mindfulness practices like meditation, journaling, or stretching in your morning routine to boost your mental clarity and reduce stress. Make it a habit to start your day with something positive before diving into your daily tasks.
Example: Spend 5 minutes each morning writing down three things you are grateful for, followed by 5 minutes of deep breathing or light stretching. This will help you cultivate a positive mindset and reduce feelings of anxiety.

3. Incorporate Regular Movement into Your Day

Regular physical activity is essential for both physical and mental well-being. Exercise not only improves your cardiovascular health and strengthens your muscles but also releases endorphins, which are natural mood boosters.

Tip: Find activities you enjoy and integrate them into your daily routine. If you're pressed for time, break your exercise into smaller chunks throughout the day. You don't need to do long, intense workouts to reap the benefits.
Example: Take a 10-minute walk during your lunch break, stretch for a few minutes after sitting for long periods, or dance to your favorite song in the morning. The key is to keep moving regularly.

4. Prioritize Sleep for Recovery and Mental Health

Getting enough sleep is crucial for physical recovery and mental well-being. Lack of sleep can lead to decreased cognitive function, mood swings, and a weakened immune system. Prioritizing good sleep hygiene can significantly improve your mental and physical health.

Tip: Create a consistent bedtime routine that helps signal to your body that it's time to wind down. Avoid screens for at least 30 minutes before bed, and create a calming environment to promote restful sleep.
Example: Develop a nightly ritual that includes activities like reading, taking a warm bath, or practicing relaxation exercises to help you relax and prepare for sleep. Aim for 7-9 hours of sleep per night, depending on your individual needs.

5. Practice Mindfulness and Stress Management

Stress is a major contributor to physical and mental health issues. Developing habits that help you manage stress and practice mindfulness can improve your emotional resilience and overall well-being.

Tip: Set aside time each day for mindfulness practices such as meditation, deep breathing, or yoga. These practices help reduce stress, improve focus, and promote a sense of calm.
Example: Dedicate 5-10 minutes daily to mindfulness exercises. You could meditate using a guided app, practice diaphragmatic breathing, or spend a few minutes focusing on your senses during a walk outside.

6. Develop Healthy Eating Habits

Nutrition plays a significant role in both your physical health and mental well-being. A balanced diet that includes whole foods, fruits, vegetables, lean proteins, and healthy fats provides the nutrients your body and brain need to function optimally.

Tip: Make small, sustainable changes to your diet rather than overhauling everything at once. Focus on adding healthy foods rather than eliminating entire food groups.

Example: Start by incorporating more vegetables into your meals—aim for half your plate to be filled with vegetables at lunch and dinner. Additionally, try to reduce your intake of processed foods and sugar, which can negatively impact your mood and energy levels.

7. Stay Hydrated for Energy and Cognitive Function

Drinking enough water throughout the day is essential for maintaining your energy levels, cognitive function, and overall health. Dehydration can lead to fatigue, difficulty concentrating, and even mood changes.

Tip: Make hydration a habit by carrying a water bottle with you wherever you go. Set reminders on your phone or use a water-tracking app to ensure you're drinking enough water.
Example: Aim to drink at least 8 cups of water per day, adjusting based on your activity level and environment. You can make this easier by associating drinking water with certain triggers, such as having a glass of water before each meal.

8. Create a Supportive Environment

Your environment plays a significant role in shaping your habits. Surrounding yourself with people, tools, and spaces that support your goals can make it easier to develop healthy habits.

Tip: Design your environment in a way that makes healthy choices easier. Remove temptations, keep healthy snacks visible, and create a space for exercise or relaxation that feels inviting.
Example: If you're trying to eat healthier, keep fruits and vegetables easily accessible in your kitchen. If you want to exercise more, keep your workout clothes and equipment in a place where you can easily grab them.

9. Cultivate Social Connections for Mental Well-Being

Strong social connections are vital for mental health. Spending time with loved ones, whether in person or virtually, can provide emotional support, reduce stress, and improve your mood.

Tip: Make an effort to stay connected with friends and family, even during busy times. Schedule regular catch-ups or activities that allow you to engage with your social circle.
Example: Set a goal to call or meet up with a friend once a week, or join a group activity like a fitness class or book club that allows you to connect with others while engaging in something enjoyable.

10. Track Your Progress and Celebrate Small Wins

Tracking your progress helps keep you accountable and allows you to see how far you've come. Celebrating small wins along the way reinforces the habit and boosts motivation.

Tip: Use a habit tracker, journal, or app to monitor your progress. Celebrate each milestone, no matter how small, to keep yourself motivated and engaged.
Example: If your goal is to meditate every day, use a habit tracker to mark off each day you complete the habit. Celebrate after completing a streak, such as 7 consecutive days of meditation.

Developing habits that promote physical and mental well-being takes time, consistency, and patience. By starting small, prioritizing key health-related behaviors, and creating an environment that supports your goals, you can cultivate habits that enhance your quality of life. Remember, the goal is progress, not perfection. Focus on making small, sustainable changes that build momentum and lead to long-term improvements in your health and well-being.

The Role of Mindfulness and Stress Management Habits

In today's fast-paced world, stress is an inevitable part of life. Whether it's caused by work, relationships, or the pressures of daily responsibilities, chronic stress can have significant negative effects on both physical and mental well-being. Developing habits centered around mindfulness and stress management can help mitigate these effects, improve emotional resilience, and enhance overall health. In this article, we will explore the role of mindfulness and stress management habits, their benefits, and how to effectively incorporate them into your daily life.

What is Mindfulness?

Mindfulness is the practice of being fully present in the moment, paying attention to your thoughts, feelings, and surroundings without judgment. It involves consciously observing what is happening both internally (e.g., your emotions and thoughts) and externally (e.g., your environment) without trying to change it. Mindfulness helps bring awareness to the present moment, which can reduce stress, increase emotional regulation, and promote a sense of calm.

Mindfulness can be practiced formally through meditation or informally by bringing mindful awareness to daily activities, such as eating, walking, or even breathing. The core of mindfulness is to stay focused on the present rather than getting caught up in worries about the future or ruminating on the past.

Benefits of Mindfulness

Mindfulness practices have been extensively studied and shown to provide numerous benefits for mental and physical health, including:

1. **Reduced Stress**: Mindfulness helps reduce stress by shifting focus away from anxious thoughts and bringing attention to the present moment. When practiced regularly, mindfulness can lower cortisol levels (the stress hormone) and create a sense of calm and relaxation.
2. **Improved Emotional Regulation**: Mindfulness helps increase self-awareness, allowing individuals to recognize their emotions before they become overwhelming. This awareness enables better emotional regulation and reduces the likelihood of reactive behaviors, such as anger or frustration.
3. **Enhanced Focus and Concentration**: Mindfulness improves attention by training the mind to focus on the present. Regular mindfulness practice can enhance cognitive function, including improved concentration and memory retention.
4. **Better Sleep**: Mindfulness practices, such as meditation, can improve sleep quality by calming the mind, reducing racing thoughts, and promoting relaxation before bed.
5. **Reduced Symptoms of Anxiety and Depression**: Mindfulness has been shown to reduce symptoms of anxiety and depression by helping individuals break the cycle of negative thought patterns. It promotes acceptance and self-compassion, which can alleviate the emotional toll of these mental health conditions.

Stress Management Habits

Stress management habits are practices or routines designed to help you cope with and reduce the negative effects of stress.

These habits help you manage both the immediate impact of stress (short-term stress relief) and the ongoing buildup of chronic stress (long-term resilience).

Effective stress management habits include a variety of activities that promote relaxation, emotional balance, and overall well-being.

Types of Stress Management Habits

1. **Mindfulness Meditation**: This is one of the most well-known and effective stress management habits. Mindfulness meditation involves sitting quietly and focusing on your breathing, bodily sensations, or a specific focal point, such as a mantra. This practice trains the mind to stay in the present, reducing stress and anxiety.

How to Practice: Set aside 5-10 minutes a day to sit in a quiet place and focus on your breathing. When your mind wanders, gently bring your attention back to your breath. Over time, increase the duration of your meditation sessions.

2. **Deep Breathing Exercises**: Deep breathing is a simple yet powerful way to reduce stress. By slowing down your breathing and taking deeper breaths, you activate the body's relaxation response, which helps lower heart rate, blood pressure, and stress levels.

How to Practice: Try diaphragmatic breathing by inhaling deeply through your nose, allowing your abdomen to expand, and then exhaling slowly through your mouth. Repeat for several minutes, especially when you feel stressed or anxious.

3. **Progressive Muscle Relaxation**: This technique involves systematically tensing and relaxing different muscle groups in the body, promoting physical and mental relaxation.

How to Practice: Starting with your feet, tense the muscles for 5 seconds, then relax for 10 seconds. Gradually work your way up through your body (legs, abdomen, arms, neck, etc.), releasing tension as you go.

4. **Journaling**: Writing about your thoughts and feelings can help reduce stress by providing an outlet for emotional expression. Journaling allows you to process your emotions, identify stressors, and gain clarity on what's troubling you.

How to Practice: Set aside 5-10 minutes each day to write about your experiences and emotions. You can focus on specific events, reflect on your feelings, or simply free-write without a particular structure.

5. **Physical Activity**: Exercise is one of the most effective stress relievers. Physical activity releases endorphins, which are natural mood elevators, and helps reduce tension and stress in the body.

How to Practice: Incorporate regular physical activity into your routine, whether it's walking, running, yoga, or any other form of exercise that you enjoy. Even short bursts of movement, like a 10-minute walk, can significantly reduce stress levels.

6. **Social Connection**: Strong social support networks help buffer against stress. Talking to a trusted friend or loved one about your challenges can help you feel supported and reduce feelings of isolation.

How to Practice: Make time to connect with friends or family members regularly. Whether it's through a phone call, video chat, or in-person interaction, engaging in supportive conversations can reduce stress.

How to Incorporate Mindfulness and Stress Management Habits into Your Daily Life

To make mindfulness and stress management habits a regular part of your routine, consider the following strategies:

1. **Start Small**: Choose one habit to focus on and practice for a few minutes each day. For example, start with 5 minutes of deep breathing or a short meditation session. Gradually increase the time as the habit

becomes more natural.
2. **Use Habit Stacking**: Attach your mindfulness or stress management practice to an existing habit. For instance, practice deep breathing after brushing your teeth in the morning or journal before going to bed.
3. **Be Consistent**: Consistency is key to seeing long-term benefits. Set aside a specific time each day for your practice and make it part of your routine, just like brushing your teeth or eating meals.
4. **Be Patient and Kind to Yourself**: Developing new habits takes time and effort. Don't expect immediate results, and be patient with yourself if you miss a day or find it difficult to focus. Treat your mindfulness and stress management practices as ongoing journeys rather than quick fixes.
5. **Celebrate Progress**: Acknowledge and celebrate the small victories along the way. Whether it's noticing that you feel calmer after meditating or that you've been more mindful during the day, positive reinforcement helps you stay motivated.

Mindfulness and stress management habits are essential tools for maintaining mental and physical well-being in a world filled with stressors. By incorporating practices such as mindfulness meditation, deep breathing, journaling, and physical activity into your daily life, you can reduce stress, enhance emotional regulation, and improve overall health. These habits not only help you manage short-term stress but also build resilience for long-term well-being. Start small, stay consistent, and gradually expand these practices to create a more balanced and mindful life.

CHAPTER 8: HABITS FOR PRODUCTIVITY AND TIME MANAGEMENT

How Habits Can Streamline Decision-Making and Increase Productivity

We make countless decisions each day, from the mundane to the significant. Each of these decisions, no matter how small, requires mental energy and cognitive resources. Over time, this accumulation of choices can lead to decision fatigue, a phenomenon where the quality of decisions deteriorates as the day progresses. One powerful way to mitigate this fatigue and boost productivity is by cultivating effective habits. Habits help automate behavior, reducing the need for conscious decision-making and freeing up mental resources for more important tasks. In this article, we'll explore how habits streamline decision-making and, in turn, increase productivity.

The Nature of Habits and Decision-Making

Habits are behaviors that are repeated regularly and tend to occur subconsciously. According to research in behavioral psychology, habits are formed through a **habit loop**, consisting of three components: a **cue** (the trigger), a **routine** (the behavior), and a **reward** (the positive reinforcement that encourages repetition). Once a habit is established, the brain no longer has to actively deliberate over the behavior—it becomes automatic.

This automation is crucial for productivity because it reduces the cognitive load of decision-making. When you rely on habits to govern certain behaviors, you no longer need to use willpower or expend energy deciding what to do next. Instead, your brain recognizes the cue and triggers the routine automatically, allowing you to focus your mental energy on more complex or creative tasks.

How Habits Streamline Decision-Making

1. Reduce Cognitive Overload

Each decision, no matter how small, uses cognitive resources. Whether it's deciding what to wear, what to eat for breakfast, or when to exercise, each choice adds to the mental load of your day. By turning these daily activities into habits, you minimize the number of decisions you need to make. This frees up mental space for more important decisions, increasing both your efficiency and effectiveness.

Example: Consider Steve Jobs, who famously wore the same type of outfit every day—a black turtleneck and jeans. By eliminating the need to decide what to wear each morning, he reduced decision fatigue and reserved his mental energy for work-related decisions.

Actionable Tip: Identify small, repetitive decisions in your daily routine and automate them by establishing consistent habits. For example, create a set morning routine that includes your outfit, breakfast, and start-of-day tasks.

2. Create Predictable Routines

Habits help create structure and predictability in your day. When you follow a routine, you know exactly what needs to be done and when, eliminating the need to repeatedly make decisions about your schedule. This reduces mental clutter and ensures that important tasks are completed consistently.

Example: Having a set routine for starting your workday, such as reviewing your to-do list, answering emails for 30 minutes, and then focusing on your most critical task, reduces the need to decide how to begin each day. This predictability not only saves mental energy but also ensures that you get started on your work quickly and efficiently.

Actionable Tip: Design routines for key parts of your day, such as your morning, work, and evening routines. Make these routines as consistent as possible so that they become automatic over time.

3. Minimize Distractions and Interruptions

Distractions are one of the biggest obstacles to productivity. When habits govern your actions, they create a kind of "autopilot" mode that helps block out distractions and focus on the task at hand. For example, if you've developed the habit of working for 90-minute blocks followed by a short break, you won't need to decide when to stop checking your email or scrolling through social media. The habit will naturally guide you toward focusing during work time and taking a break afterward.

Example: Implementing a habit of using the **Pomodoro Technique**—working for 25-minute intervals followed by 5-minute breaks—helps minimize distractions because you know exactly when you'll take your next break. This reduces the temptation to check your phone or engage in other unproductive activities.

Actionable Tip: Use time-blocking or the Pomodoro Technique to structure your workday into focused intervals, making it easier to stay on task without constantly deliberating when to start or stop.

4. Conserve Willpower for Important Decisions

Willpower is a finite resource. Each time you exert willpower to make a decision or resist temptation, you deplete this resource. By relying on habits, you reduce the number of decisions that require willpower, allowing you to conserve it for more critical choices or challenging tasks.

Example: If you've built the habit of going to the gym at the same time every morning, you no longer need to rely on willpower to decide whether or not to exercise. The habit kicks in automatically, preserving your willpower for other tasks later in the day.

Actionable Tip: Automate as many behaviors as possible—such as exercise, meal planning, and bedtime routines—so you can save your willpower for more demanding tasks, such as solving problems at work or making important life decisions.

How Habits Increase Productivity

1. **Build Momentum and Consistency**

When you establish habits, they create momentum. The consistent performance of these behaviors day after day builds confidence, reduces procrastination, and leads to a cumulative effect on your productivity. The more ingrained the habit becomes, the less effort it takes to maintain it, allowing you to accomplish more in less time.

Example: Developing a habit of setting daily priorities before you start work helps you focus on the most important tasks right from the start. Over time, this consistent prioritization will improve your productivity by ensuring that you're always working on high-impact activities.

Actionable Tip: Start your day with a habit of writing down your top three priorities. This habit will help you consistently focus on what matters most, making your work more efficient and effective.

2. **Increase Focus and Flow**

Habits help you enter a state of **flow**, where you become fully immersed in a task with heightened focus and concentration. When habits automate certain behaviors, you can move seamlessly from one task to the next without overthinking or hesitating. This ability to focus deeply leads to greater productivity and higher-quality work.

Example: If you've built a habit of spending the first two hours of your workday in deep work—free from distractions—you'll be able to achieve a flow state more easily. This increased focus allows you to complete complex tasks faster and with better results.

Actionable Tip: Set aside dedicated time blocks each day for deep work or focused tasks. Make this a habit by consistently working during the same time period each day, helping you get into a flow state more easily.

3. Eliminate Procrastination

Procrastination often occurs when you're unsure of where to start or what to do next. Habits remove the need to deliberate over these decisions, making it easier to get started and avoid procrastination. Once a behavior becomes a habit, you're less likely to put it off because it feels natural to engage in it.

Example: If you develop a habit of tackling your hardest task first thing in the morning (known as "eating the frog"), you'll eliminate procrastination around that task. Completing it early in the day will give you a sense of accomplishment and set a productive tone for the rest of your day.

Actionable Tip: Identify one key habit to help you overcome procrastination, such as starting your day with the most challenging task. Commit to this habit until it becomes second nature, reducing the tendency to delay important work.

Habits are powerful tools for streamlining decision-making and boosting productivity. By automating repetitive behaviors and reducing cognitive overload, habits allow you to focus on what truly matters, conserve mental energy, and minimize distractions. Developing consistent routines, conserving willpower, and eliminating procrastination through habit formation can lead to increased productivity, better decision-making, and a more efficient use of your time. The key is to start small, build momentum, and let your habits work for you, freeing your mind to tackle the bigger challenges in life.

Exploring Time Management Techniques: The Pomodoro Technique, Time Blocking, and Daily Planning

Effective time management is crucial for staying productive, achieving goals, and maintaining a work-life balance. With the growing demands of work and personal responsibilities, it's easy to feel overwhelmed or stretched too thin. However, using proven time management techniques can help you organize your day, focus on the right tasks, and make the most of your time. This article explores three powerful time management techniques—the Pomodoro Technique, time blocking, and daily planning—and how they can help you maximize productivity and reduce stress.

1. The Pomodoro Technique

The **Pomodoro Technique** is a time management method developed by Francesco Cirillo in the late 1980s. It is based on breaking your work into focused intervals, traditionally 25 minutes long, called **Pomodoros**, followed by short breaks. The technique is designed to increase focus and minimize distractions, allowing you to work more efficiently without feeling overwhelmed.

How the Pomodoro Technique Works

1. **Choose a Task**: Select the task you want to work on.
2. **Set a Timer**: Set a timer for 25 minutes (one Pomodoro).
3. **Work Focused**: Work on the task with full concentration until the timer rings. Avoid

interruptions during this time.
4. **Take a Short Break**: Once the timer rings, take a 5-minute break. Step away from your workspace, stretch, or relax.
5. **Repeat**: After completing four Pomodoros, take a longer break (15-30 minutes) to rest and recharge.

Benefits of the Pomodoro Technique

Increases Focus: By working in short, focused bursts, you minimize distractions and train your brain to stay engaged in the task at hand.
Reduces Mental Fatigue: The built-in breaks help prevent burnout and mental exhaustion, keeping you energized throughout the day.
Improves Task Completion: The sense of urgency created by the timer encourages you to work efficiently and complete tasks within each Pomodoro.
Enhances Time Awareness: The technique helps you become more aware of how you spend your time and how long tasks take to complete.

Tips for Implementing the Pomodoro Technique

Start with the traditional 25-minute Pomodoro and adjust the timing based on your preferences and the nature of your work. Some people prefer longer intervals (e.g., 45-50 minutes) followed by slightly longer breaks.
Use a Pomodoro timer app (such as Focus Booster or Pomodone) to automate your intervals and keep track of your work sessions.
If you're interrupted during a Pomodoro, jot down the distraction and come back to it after the session is complete.

2. Time Blocking

Time blocking is a time management technique that involves scheduling specific blocks of time for different tasks or activities throughout the day. Rather than working from a to-do list and hoping to get everything done, you allocate dedicated time slots for each task on your calendar. Time blocking helps you prioritize your tasks, minimize multitasking, and maintain focus on one activity at a time.

How Time Blocking Works

1. **Identify Your Tasks**: List the tasks you need to complete for the day or week.
2. **Create Time Blocks**: Allocate specific time slots for each task on your calendar. For example, block off 9:00 AM - 10:30 AM for focused work on a specific project, followed by 30 minutes for responding to emails.
3. **Stick to the Schedule**: During each time block, focus solely on the task assigned to that block. Avoid switching tasks or multitasking during this period.
4. **Review and Adjust**: At the end of the day or week, review your time blocks and adjust them if necessary. Ensure that your time is being allocated effectively based on your priorities.

Benefits of Time Blocking

Boosts Focus and Productivity: By dedicating specific time slots to each task, time blocking encourages deep work and helps you avoid distractions.

Prioritizes Important Tasks: Time blocking forces you to think about your priorities and allocate time to the tasks that matter most.

Reduces Multitasking: Focusing on one task at a time reduces the mental cost of switching between tasks, which can improve the quality of your work.

Increases Accountability: With a set schedule in place, you are more likely to stay on track and complete tasks within the designated time frame.

Tips for Effective Time Blocking

Begin by blocking time for high-priority tasks during your most productive hours (e.g., morning for deep work) and allocate time for less demanding tasks (e.g., email, meetings) during lower-energy periods.
Leave some buffer time between blocks to accommodate unexpected tasks or delays.
Consider blocking off time for self-care, breaks, and personal activities to ensure a well-rounded schedule.

3. Daily Planning

Daily planning involves setting clear goals and organizing your day around those goals. It helps you focus on what's most important, ensuring that you're not just busy, but productive. By taking a few minutes each morning (or the night before) to plan your day, you can approach your tasks with greater clarity and purpose.

How Daily Planning Works

1. **Set Your Priorities**: Identify the top 3-5 tasks that are most important to complete that day. These should align with your broader goals and have a significant impact on your progress.
2. **Organize Your Tasks**: Arrange your tasks in order of priority. Begin with the most important or challenging task first (often referred to as "eating the frog"), and work your way through the rest of the list.
3. **Allocate Time**: Estimate how much time each task will take and plan when you will work on each task throughout the day.
4. **Review and Adjust**: At the end of the day, review what you accomplished, reflect on what worked well, and adjust your plan for the next day accordingly.

Benefits of Daily Planning

Clarifies Goals: Daily planning helps you clarify your goals and

ensures that your tasks are aligned with your priorities.
Enhances Focus: By organizing your day around your most important tasks, you reduce the risk of getting sidetracked by less important activities.
Improves Time Management: Planning your day helps you manage your time more effectively, reducing wasted time and improving overall productivity.
Promotes Reflection and Learning: Regularly reviewing your daily progress helps you identify areas for improvement and learn from your experiences.

Tips for Effective Daily Planning

Plan your day the night before to start the next day with a clear sense of purpose.

Use a planner, notebook, or app to organize your tasks and time allocations.

Prioritize your tasks by importance and urgency, and tackle the most challenging tasks early in the day when your energy is highest.

The Pomodoro Technique, time blocking, and daily planning are powerful time management strategies that can significantly improve your productivity and reduce stress. The Pomodoro Technique helps break tasks into manageable intervals, promoting focus and minimizing distractions. Time blocking structures your day, ensuring that each task gets dedicated attention, while daily planning allows you to prioritize your most important tasks and approach your day with clarity and purpose.

By incorporating these techniques into your routine, you can streamline your workflow, reduce decision fatigue, and create a more balanced, productive day. Whether you're managing a busy work schedule or balancing multiple responsibilities, these time management tools can help you make the most of your time and achieve your goals with greater efficiency.

Examples of Productivity Habits from Successful People

Productivity habits are crucial for achieving success, especially for individuals who manage multiple demands and responsibilities. Successful people across various industries have adopted specific routines and habits that allow them to maintain high levels of productivity while still pursuing personal and professional growth. In this article, we'll explore some of the productivity habits used by highly successful people and how you can apply them to your own life.

1. The Morning Routine - Tim Cook (Apple CEO)

One of the most common habits among successful people is the implementation of a **structured morning routine**. Tim Cook, the CEO of Apple, is known for waking up at 4:00 AM to get a head start on the day. He begins by reading and responding to emails, followed by a workout to boost his energy levels for the day ahead. Cook's disciplined morning routine sets the tone for the rest of his day, allowing him to maintain focus and productivity.

Why It Works: Morning routines provide a consistent structure that helps eliminate decision fatigue early in the day. By establishing a routine, successful people can start their day on a positive, productive note, while also ensuring that important tasks like exercise or planning are addressed first.

How You Can Apply It: Design a morning routine that includes activities to prepare you mentally and physically for the day ahead. This could involve exercising, reading, journaling, meditating, or simply setting goals for the day. The key is to make it consistent and tailored to your needs.

2. Time Blocking - Elon Musk (Tesla and SpaceX CEO)

Elon Musk is famous for his rigorous use of **time blocking** to manage his busy schedule. Musk breaks his day into five-minute intervals, each dedicated to specific tasks. Whether he's working on product development at Tesla or leading engineering efforts at SpaceX, Musk ensures that every minute is accounted for. This level of structure allows him to balance multiple complex projects without getting overwhelmed.

Why It Works: Time blocking forces you to allocate specific periods for tasks, which helps eliminate distractions and ensures that you're fully focused on the task at hand. It also helps you set boundaries and avoid spending too much time on low-priority activities.

How You Can Apply It: Start by breaking your day into blocks of time dedicated to different tasks or categories of work. This could be 30-minute or one-hour blocks depending on your workload. Assign specific activities to each block, such as deep work, meetings, or personal time, and stick to the schedule as closely as possible.

3. The "Two-Minute Rule" - David Allen (Author of *Getting Things Done*)

David Allen, the productivity guru behind the popular *Getting Things Done* (GTD) methodology, advocates for the **Two-Minute Rule**. This rule states that if a task takes less than two minutes to complete, you should do it immediately rather than putting it off. Allen believes this simple rule prevents small tasks from piling up and helps maintain momentum throughout the day.

Why It Works: The Two-Minute Rule minimizes procrastination and ensures that minor tasks don't accumulate and create unnecessary stress. By completing these small tasks right away, you can keep your workflow clean and focused on larger, more important projects.

How You Can Apply It: Incorporate the Two-Minute Rule into your daily routine. If an email, phone call, or minor task takes less than two minutes, handle it immediately rather than adding it to your to-do list. This will help keep your list of pending tasks manageable and prevent small distractions from derailing your focus.

4. Deep Work - Cal Newport (Author of *Deep Work*)

Cal Newport, author of *Deep Work: Rules for Focused Success in a Distracted World*, champions the concept of **deep work**, which involves dedicating long periods to undistracted, focused work on cognitively demanding tasks. Newport believes that deep work is crucial for producing high-quality work and achieving breakthroughs in any field.

Why It Works: Deep work maximizes cognitive abilities and allows you to make significant progress on complex tasks. By minimizing distractions and interruptions, you can enter a state of flow, where productivity is at its peak.

How You Can Apply It: Set aside dedicated time blocks for deep work each day. Turn off distractions like email, social media, and notifications during these periods. Ideally, aim for at least 90 minutes of uninterrupted focus on your most important tasks. Start small and gradually increase the amount of time you dedicate to deep work as you build your focus.

5. Prioritizing Health and Fitness - Richard Branson (Founder of Virgin Group)

Richard Branson, the founder of the Virgin Group, is a firm believer in the importance of **exercise for productivity**. Branson starts his day with physical activity, whether it's running, swimming, or playing tennis. He credits his active lifestyle for boosting his energy levels and improving his focus and mood, allowing him to remain productive throughout the day.

Why It Works: Exercise is a proven way to boost cognitive function, increase energy, and reduce stress. When you prioritize your physical health, you're better equipped to handle the demands of your work and life, resulting in higher productivity and improved well-being.

How You Can Apply It: Incorporate exercise into your daily routine, whether it's a morning workout, a lunchtime walk, or a yoga session after work. Even 20-30 minutes of physical activity can make a significant difference in your energy levels and mental clarity.

6. Daily Planning - Benjamin Franklin (Founding Father and Inventor)

Benjamin Franklin was known for his commitment to **daily planning**. He would start his day by asking himself, "What good shall I do this day?" and then plan out his tasks accordingly. Franklin believed that structuring his day in advance allowed him to make the most of his time, ensuring that he stayed productive and focused on his goals.

Why It Works: Daily planning provides clarity and direction for the day ahead. By setting clear intentions and outlining your tasks, you can prioritize what matters most and stay on track throughout the day.

How You Can Apply It: Start each morning (or the night before) by setting your priorities for the day. Identify the key tasks you need to accomplish and plan when and how you will tackle them. Review your progress at the end of the day to assess what worked and what didn't.

7. Single Tasking - Oprah Winfrey (Media Mogul and Entrepreneur)

Oprah Winfrey is a proponent of **single tasking**, which involves focusing on one task at a time rather than multitasking. She believes that giving full attention to one task allows her to work more efficiently and produce higher-quality results. Single-tasking also reduces stress and helps create a sense of accomplishment after completing each task.

Why It Works: Multitasking often leads to diminished focus and lower productivity because your brain has to constantly switch between tasks. Single-tasking allows you to immerse yourself fully in one activity, improving both the quality and speed of your work.

How You Can Apply It: Focus on one task at a time, and avoid trying to juggle multiple activities simultaneously. Set aside dedicated time for each task and give it your full attention until it's completed before moving on to the next.

The productivity habits of successful people share common themes: focus, discipline, consistency, and prioritization. From implementing structured morning routines like Tim Cook to using time blocking like Elon Musk, these habits help successful individuals manage their time effectively and maximize their output. By incorporating habits such as deep work, daily planning, exercise, and single-tasking, you too can enhance your productivity and work towards achieving your goals with greater efficiency and focus.

CHAPTER 9: SOCIAL HABITS: BUILDING STRONG RELATIONSHIPS

The Role of Habits in Creating and Maintaining Personal and Professional Relationships

Habits play a crucial role in shaping our lives, not only in terms of productivity, health, and personal growth, but also in the quality of our relationships. Both personal and professional relationships require regular attention, communication, and care to flourish, and habits help make these efforts consistent and sustainable. By developing and maintaining positive habits, we can strengthen our connections with others, build trust, and foster deeper bonds that last over time. This article explores the role of habits in creating and maintaining both personal and professional relationships.

1. Consistency and Reliability

In relationships, consistency is key to building trust and reliability. Whether it's showing up for family dinners, regularly checking in with friends, or following through on work commitments, habits help ensure that your interactions are predictable and dependable.

Personal Relationships

In personal relationships, consistency helps create a sense of security and stability. For example, regularly setting aside time to spend with your partner, such as weekly date nights or daily check-ins, can strengthen the bond and maintain emotional intimacy. Similarly, maintaining the habit of reaching out to friends or family members on a regular basis fosters connection and ensures that your relationships remain active, even during busy periods.

Example: A simple habit like texting or calling a friend every

Sunday to catch up can help sustain the relationship, even when life gets hectic. This regular check-in helps maintain closeness and shows that you value the relationship.

Professional Relationships

In professional relationships, consistency builds credibility and trust. Developing habits like responding to emails promptly, meeting deadlines, and regularly updating colleagues or clients creates a reputation for reliability. This fosters stronger professional relationships because people know they can count on you to deliver consistently.

Example: A habit of sending regular updates to your manager or team at the end of the week helps ensure that communication remains open and transparent. This not only strengthens your professional relationships but also demonstrates accountability and dedication.

2. Effective Communication

Communication is the foundation of any successful relationship. Establishing habits that promote clear, respectful, and regular communication can prevent misunderstandings, resolve conflicts, and deepen connections.

Personal Relationships

In personal relationships, the habit of **active listening** is essential. This involves giving your full attention to the other person when they are speaking, acknowledging their feelings, and responding thoughtfully. Making a habit of checking in with your partner or loved ones, asking how their day went, or discussing important topics openly helps to foster emotional intimacy and prevent feelings of disconnection.

Example: A daily habit of spending 10-15 minutes in meaningful conversation with your partner after work—free from distractions like phones or TV—can help maintain a strong emotional connection and provide a safe space to discuss any concerns or feelings.

Professional Relationships

In professional settings, communication habits such as **clarifying expectations**, **asking for feedback**, and **expressing gratitude** play a crucial role in maintaining positive relationships. Regularly checking in with your colleagues or team, ensuring that everyone is on the same page, and offering constructive feedback builds rapport and prevents potential conflicts or miscommunications.

Example: A habit of providing clear and concise email communication—summarizing key points, next steps, and deadlines—can reduce misunderstandings and improve collaboration with colleagues.

3. Empathy and Understanding

Empathy is a vital component of healthy relationships. Developing the habit of practicing empathy—actively considering the perspectives and feelings of others—can lead to more supportive and compassionate relationships, both personally and professionally.

Personal Relationships

Empathy strengthens personal relationships by helping you understand and relate to the emotions of your loved ones. Habits like validating your partner's feelings during difficult conversations or regularly checking in on a friend's well-being show that you care about their experiences and are willing to offer support.

Example: If a friend is going through a tough time, the habit of sending encouraging messages or simply listening to them when they need to vent demonstrates empathy and emotional support. This helps build deeper trust and connection.

Professional Relationships

In the workplace, practicing empathy fosters stronger professional relationships by promoting a positive and supportive work environment. This could involve regularly acknowledging the challenges your coworkers face, offering help when needed, or recognizing their contributions. When empathy becomes a habit, it encourages a culture of collaboration and mutual respect.

Example: The habit of regularly thanking colleagues for their contributions to a project, or offering assistance when they are under pressure, demonstrates empathy and can improve teamwork and morale.

4. Boundaries and Respect

Healthy relationships, whether personal or professional, require clear boundaries and mutual respect. Developing habits that reinforce respect for others' time, space, and emotional needs can prevent misunderstandings and promote healthier interactions.

Personal Relationships

In personal relationships, habits like **respecting each other's time**, **avoiding interrupting during conversations**, and **communicating needs and boundaries clearly** help ensure that both parties feel valued and respected. For example, creating a habit of discussing and respecting each other's boundaries around alone time or socializing can prevent resentment or conflict.

Example: A habit of scheduling weekly check-ins to discuss any concerns or boundaries within a relationship helps ensure that both parties feel heard and understood, leading to a healthier and more respectful dynamic.

Professional Relationships

In professional relationships, habits like **respecting others' work hours, being punctual,** and **acknowledging boundaries around communication (e.g., not contacting colleagues outside of work hours)** are essential for maintaining professionalism and respect. These habits contribute to a positive work environment where boundaries are honored, reducing stress and promoting productivity.

Example: The habit of scheduling meetings during work hours and avoiding after-hours communication unless necessary shows respect for your colleagues' personal time and fosters healthier professional boundaries.

5. Accountability and Follow-Through

Accountability is critical in both personal and professional relationships. Establishing habits of follow-through—doing what you say you will do—strengthens trust and reinforces your reliability.

Personal Relationships

In personal relationships, following through on promises and commitments is crucial for building trust and maintaining a strong bond. The habit of keeping your word—whether it's showing up for a planned outing, sticking to a commitment, or being there during tough times—demonstrates that you value the relationship.

Example: A habit of consistently following through on planned activities with friends or family members, like attending weekly dinners or outings, reinforces the importance of the relationship and builds trust.

Professional Relationships

In professional settings, habits that demonstrate accountability, such as meeting deadlines, delivering on promises, and taking responsibility for your actions, help build credibility and trust with colleagues, clients, and supervisors.

Example: A habit of sending a follow-up email after meetings to confirm agreed-upon actions and deadlines shows accountability and helps build a reputation for reliability and professionalism.

Habits are the building blocks of strong and enduring relationships, both personal and professional. By cultivating habits centered on consistency, communication, empathy, respect, and accountability, you can create deeper connections, build trust, and maintain healthy, fulfilling relationships. Whether it's scheduling regular check-ins with a partner or delivering on work commitments, these habits foster positive interactions and ensure that relationships remain strong over time.

Habits That Foster Empathy, Communication, and Trust

Empathy, communication, and trust are the cornerstones of any strong relationship, whether personal or professional. These elements are essential for understanding others, expressing ourselves clearly, and building reliable, lasting connections. Developing habits that nurture empathy, enhance communication, and build trust can significantly improve the quality of our relationships. This article explores specific habits that can help you cultivate these vital qualities.

1. Active Listening: The Foundation of Empathy and Communication

Active listening is one of the most important habits for fostering empathy and improving communication. It involves fully focusing on the speaker, understanding their message, and responding thoughtfully. Unlike passive listening, where one might only hear words without fully engaging, active listening requires conscious effort and attentiveness.

How to Practice Active Listening:

Give Your Full Attention: Put away distractions, such as your phone or laptop, and focus entirely on the person speaking. Maintain eye contact and show that you are engaged.
Acknowledge the Speaker: Use verbal and non-verbal cues, such as nodding, saying "I see" or "I understand," to show that you are following along.
Reflect and Clarify: Summarize what the speaker has said to ensure you understand their message correctly. Ask clarifying questions if something isn't clear.
Respond Thoughtfully: Take a moment to consider your response before speaking. Make sure your reply is considerate and directly related to what was discussed.

Why It Works: Active listening fosters empathy by helping you truly understand the other person's perspective. It also enhances communication by ensuring that both parties are on the same page, reducing the likelihood of misunderstandings. Over time, consistently practicing active listening builds trust, as people feel heard and valued in your presence.

2. Expressing Appreciation Regularly

Expressing appreciation is a powerful habit that builds trust and strengthens relationships. Regularly acknowledging and valuing others' efforts, whether in a personal or professional setting, reinforces positive behavior and deepens emotional connections.

How to Express Appreciation:

Be Specific: Rather than giving generic compliments, be specific about what you appreciate. For example, instead of saying "Good job," say, "I really appreciate how you handled that difficult situation with such patience and tact."

Show Gratitude Often: Make it a habit to express gratitude regularly, not just for big gestures but also for small, everyday actions. This could be as simple as thanking a colleague for their help on a project or appreciating your partner for their support.

Use Various Forms of Expression: Appreciation can be expressed verbally, through written notes or emails, or by small acts of kindness. The key is to make the other person feel valued.

Why It Works: Expressing appreciation fosters trust by making people feel recognized and valued. It also strengthens communication by creating a positive atmosphere where people are more likely to share openly. When others know you appreciate them, they are more inclined to trust you and continue contributing positively to the relationship.

3. Practicing Empathy Through Perspective-Taking

Perspective-taking is a habit that involves putting yourself in someone else's shoes to understand their feelings, thoughts, and motivations. This habit helps cultivate empathy, allowing you to connect with others on a deeper level.

How to Practice Perspective-Taking:

Pause and Reflect: When someone shares their experience or emotions with you, take a moment to reflect on what it might be like to be in their situation. Consider their background, challenges, and feelings.

Ask Open-Ended Questions: Encourage others to share more about their experiences by asking open-ended questions, such as "How did that make you feel?" or "What was that like for you?"

Avoid Judgments: Practice withholding judgment and focus on understanding rather than evaluating or offering solutions immediately.

Why It Works: Perspective-taking deepens your empathy by helping you appreciate the complexities of others' experiences. It also improves communication by encouraging open dialogue and reducing misunderstandings. Over time, this habit builds trust as people feel you genuinely understand and care about their experiences.

4. Maintaining Open and Honest Communication

Open and honest communication is crucial for building trust in any relationship. It involves being transparent about your thoughts, feelings, and intentions, and encouraging others to do the same. This habit requires a commitment to clarity and authenticity in all interactions.

How to Practice Open and Honest Communication:

Be Transparent: Share your thoughts, feelings, and concerns openly with others. Avoid hiding or downplaying important information, even if it's uncomfortable to discuss.

Encourage Openness in Others: Create a safe space for others to express themselves by being non-judgmental and supportive when they share their thoughts or feelings.

Address Issues Directly: If there's a problem or conflict, address it directly rather than letting it fester. Use "I" statements to express how you feel and what you need, without blaming the other person.

Why It Works: Open and honest communication builds trust by fostering transparency and reducing the potential for misunderstandings or hidden resentments. When people know they can count on you to be truthful and straightforward, they are more likely to trust you and engage in meaningful conversations.

5. Consistently Following Through on Commitments

Following through on commitments is a habit that directly builds trust. Whether it's personal promises or professional obligations, consistently doing what you say you will do shows that you are reliable and trustworthy.

How to Put this into Practice:

Be Realistic About Commitments: Only commit to what you know you can deliver. Avoid overpromising and underdelivering, as this can damage trust.
Set Reminders: Use reminders, calendars, or to-do lists to ensure you don't forget your commitments. Prioritize following through, even on small tasks.
Communicate If There Are Delays: If you're unable to meet a commitment on time, communicate this as soon as possible and provide a clear plan for when you can fulfill it.

Why It Works: Following through on commitments builds trust by demonstrating that you are dependable. It also strengthens communication by ensuring that expectations are clear and met consistently. Over time, this habit establishes a reputation for reliability, which is essential for strong, trusting relationships.

6. Apologizing and Making Amends When Necessary

Apologizing when you've made a mistake or hurt someone is a habit that fosters both empathy and trust. A genuine apology shows that you recognize your impact on others and are committed to making things right.

How to Apologize Effectively:

Acknowledge the Impact: Recognize and acknowledge how your actions affected the other person. Be specific about what

you are apologizing for.
Take Responsibility: Avoid making excuses or deflecting blame. Take full responsibility for your actions.
Make Amends: Offer a way to make things right, whether it's by changing your behavior, offering a solution, or simply listening to the other person's feelings.

Why It Works: Apologizing and making amends builds trust by showing that you are accountable for your actions and committed to maintaining a healthy relationship. It also fosters empathy by acknowledging the other person's feelings and taking steps to address them.

Habits that foster empathy, communication, and trust are essential for building and maintaining strong relationships. Active listening, expressing appreciation, practicing perspective-taking, maintaining open and honest communication, following through on commitments, and apologizing when necessary are all habits that can significantly enhance the quality of your personal and professional connections. By cultivating these habits, you create an environment of mutual respect, understanding, and reliability, which are the foundations of lasting and meaningful relationships.

Strategies for Building Better Habits in Social Interactions

Social interactions are a fundamental part of our daily lives, influencing both personal and professional relationships. The quality of these interactions often depends on the habits we develop over time—whether we are aware of them or not. Building better habits in social interactions can enhance communication, foster deeper connections, and create more positive experiences for everyone involved. This article explores effective strategies for cultivating better habits in social interactions.

1. Practice Active Listening

Active listening is one of the most powerful habits you can develop in social interactions. It involves fully focusing on the speaker, understanding their message, and responding thoughtfully. By practicing active listening, you show respect and empathy, making others feel heard and valued.

How to Practice Active Listening:

Give Your Full Attention: Avoid distractions when someone is speaking. This means putting away your phone, maintaining eye contact, and focusing on the conversation.
Use Verbal and Non-Verbal Cues: Show that you are engaged by nodding, making affirmative sounds like "I see" or "Uh-huh," and maintaining an open body posture.
Reflect and Clarify: Summarize what the other person has said to ensure you've understood correctly, and ask clarifying questions if necessary.
Avoid Interrupting: Let the speaker finish their thoughts before you respond. Interrupting can disrupt the flow of conversation and make the speaker feel undervalued.

Example: If a friend is sharing a personal story, practice active listening by putting aside your thoughts or opinions and focusing entirely on what they're saying. Reflect their emotions back to them by saying something like, "It sounds like that was really challenging for you."

2. Cultivate Empathy Through Perspective-Taking

Empathy is the ability to understand and share the feelings of others. Developing the habit of empathy through perspective-taking can greatly improve your social interactions, making you more compassionate and understanding in your responses.

How to Cultivate Empathy:

Pause and Reflect: Before reacting, take a moment to consider what the other person might be experiencing. Imagine yourself in their situation and think about how you would feel.
Ask Open-Ended Questions: Encourage the other person to share more about their feelings or experiences by asking questions like, "How did that affect you?" or "What was that like for you?"
Validate Their Feelings: Acknowledge the other person's emotions, even if you don't fully understand or agree with their perspective. Validation shows that you respect their feelings and view them as legitimate.

Example: When a coworker expresses frustration over a project, instead of dismissing their feelings, you might say, "I can see why that would be frustrating. It sounds like it's been a tough situation." This approach fosters a more empathetic and supportive interaction.

3. Focus on Positive Body Language

Non-verbal communication plays a significant role in social interactions. Your body language can convey openness, confidence, and attentiveness—or it can send signals of disinterest or discomfort. Developing positive body language habits can enhance the way others perceive you and improve the quality of your interactions.

How to Develop Positive Body Language:

Maintain Eye Contact: Eye contact shows that you are engaged and interested in the conversation. Aim for balanced eye contact—too much can be intimidating, but too little can seem disengaged.
Smile: A genuine smile can make you appear more approachable and friendly. It can also help put others at ease.

Use Open Posture: Keep your posture open and relaxed. Avoid crossing your arms or legs, as this can signal defensiveness or discomfort.

Mirror the Other Person's Body Language: Subtly mirroring the other person's gestures or posture can create a sense of connection and rapport.

Example: During a job interview, maintain eye contact with the interviewer, smile when appropriate, and keep your posture open and relaxed. This non-verbal communication reinforces your verbal responses and helps create a positive impression.

4. Practice Thoughtful Communication

Thoughtful communication involves being mindful of how your words and actions affect others. It's about choosing your words carefully, considering the other person's perspective, and aiming to communicate clearly and respectfully.

How to Practice Thoughtful Communication:

Think Before You Speak: Take a moment to consider how your words might be received. Avoid making impulsive or emotionally charged statements that you might regret later.

Be Clear and Concise: Avoid ambiguity by expressing your thoughts clearly and directly. This reduces the risk of misunderstandings and ensures that your message is understood as intended.

Use "I" Statements: When discussing sensitive topics, use "I" statements to express your feelings without blaming or criticizing the other person. For example, "I felt overlooked when my contributions weren't acknowledged" rather than "You never give me credit."

Avoid Gossip and Negative Talk: Refrain from speaking negatively about others, as it can create a toxic environment and damage relationships. Focus on positive or constructive discussions instead.

Example: If you need to provide feedback to a team member, use thoughtful communication by framing your comments in a way that is constructive and supportive. For instance, "I noticed that the project deadline was missed. Let's discuss how we can manage our time better in the future to ensure we stay on track."

5. Set Boundaries and Respect Others' Boundaries

Healthy social interactions often require clear boundaries. Setting and respecting boundaries helps prevent misunderstandings, reduces stress, and fosters mutual respect in relationships.

How to Set and Respect Boundaries:

Communicate Your Boundaries Clearly: Let others know your limits in a respectful and straightforward way. For example, if you need personal time after work, communicate this to your colleagues or family members.
Respect Others' Boundaries: When someone sets a boundary, honor it without trying to push or test their limits. This shows respect for their needs and builds trust in the relationship.
Be Consistent: Consistently enforcing your boundaries and respecting others' boundaries helps establish clear expectations and reduces the likelihood of conflict.

Example: If a friend frequently calls you late at night and it disrupts your sleep, you might say, "I appreciate our conversations, but I need to get to bed earlier these days. Can we catch up earlier in the evening instead?" This sets a clear boundary while maintaining the relationship.

6. Follow Through on Commitments

Reliability is a key component of trust in social interactions. Developing the habit of following through on your commitments—whether big or small—builds credibility and strengthens your relationships.

How to Follow Through:

Be Selective with Commitments: Only commit to what you know you can realistically deliver. It's better to under-promise and over-deliver than to make commitments you can't keep.
Use Reminders: Keep track of your commitments using tools like calendars, to-do lists, or reminder apps. This ensures you don't forget important tasks or promises.
Communicate If You Can't Fulfill a Commitment: If circumstances prevent you from following through, communicate this as soon as possible and offer an alternative solution.

Example: If you've promised to help a friend move, make sure you set aside the necessary time and follow through on the commitment. If something comes up that prevents you from helping, let them know as early as possible and see if you can assist in another way.

Building better habits in social interactions can significantly enhance the quality of your relationships and improve the way you connect with others. By practicing active listening, cultivating empathy, focusing on positive body language, communicating thoughtfully, setting and respecting boundaries, and following through on commitments, you can create more meaningful and effective interactions. These habits not only make you a better communicator but also help you build stronger, more trusting relationships in both personal and professional contexts.

CHAPTER 10: THE LONG GAME: TURNING HABITS INTO A LIFESTYLE

The Importance of Making Habits a Long-Term Lifestyle Rather Than a Short-Term Fix

In our fast-paced world, it's easy to seek quick fixes and short-term solutions for problems, especially when it comes to self-improvement. Whether it's crash diets, intense but unsustainable workout plans, or fleeting attempts at better time management, many people approach habit formation with a short-term mindset. However, making habits a long-term lifestyle rather than a temporary fix is crucial for achieving lasting success and well-being. This article explores why adopting a long-term perspective on habits is essential and how it can lead to more meaningful and sustained change.

1. Sustainability and Consistency

One of the primary reasons to focus on making habits a part of your long-term lifestyle is sustainability. Short-term fixes often rely on intense, unsustainable efforts that can lead to burnout, frustration, or eventual abandonment of the habit. On the other hand, long-term habits are designed to be sustainable —they are integrated into your daily routine in a way that feels manageable and consistent over time.

Why Sustainability Matters:

Prevents Burnout: When you adopt a habit as a short-term fix, you might start with enthusiasm and intensity. However, this can quickly lead to burnout if the habit is not sustainable. For example, adopting a rigorous exercise regimen that leaves no room for rest days may lead to physical and mental exhaustion, making it harder to maintain over time.

Encourages Consistency: Long-term habits are built around consistency rather than intensity. This consistency is key to forming a habit that sticks. Small, consistent actions are more likely to become ingrained in your routine and can lead to significant results over time.

Example: Instead of adopting a restrictive diet for rapid weight loss, focus on gradually incorporating healthy eating habits into your daily life. This might involve making small changes, like adding more vegetables to your meals or reducing sugar intake, which are easier to maintain long-term and contribute to lasting health benefits.

2. Building a Strong Foundation

Long-term habits are like the building blocks of your lifestyle. By focusing on gradual, sustainable changes, you create a strong foundation for your overall well-being. This foundation supports not only the specific habit you're working on but also other areas of your life.

How Long-Term Habits Build a Strong Foundation:

Promote Holistic Growth: When you approach habits as part of a long-term lifestyle, you're more likely to see positive changes in multiple areas of your life. For instance, developing a regular exercise habit not only improves physical health but can also enhance mental clarity, reduce stress, and boost confidence.
Create Positive Ripple Effects: Long-term habits often lead to other positive behaviors. For example, establishing a habit of going to bed early might improve your sleep quality, which in turn enhances your mood, energy levels, and productivity the next day.

Example: Building a habit of daily mindfulness meditation can create a ripple effect in your life. By taking just 10 minutes a day to meditate, you may find that you're more focused at work, better able to manage stress, and more patient in your relationships.

3. Encouraging Lasting Change

The goal of habit formation should be to create lasting change, not just temporary results. Short-term fixes often fail because they don't address the underlying behaviors or mindsets that need to change. Long-term habits, however, are focused on transforming these deeper aspects of your life, leading to enduring improvements.

Why Lasting Change Is Important:

Addresses Root Causes: Long-term habits require you to dig deeper into why you want to make a change and how you can sustain it. This introspection helps you address the root causes of unhealthy behaviors, rather than just treating the symptoms.

Fosters Identity Change: When you commit to a habit as part of your long-term lifestyle, it becomes part of your identity. For example, instead of just "trying to eat healthy," you start to see yourself as someone who values nutrition and wellness, which makes it easier to maintain the habit.

Example: If you're trying to improve your financial habits, a short-term fix might involve cutting out all discretionary spending for a month. While this can lead to temporary savings, it doesn't address the underlying spending habits. A long-term approach might involve setting a realistic budget, tracking your expenses, and gradually shifting your spending habits over time, leading to lasting financial stability.

4. Reducing the Pressure of Perfection

Short-term fixes often come with the pressure to be perfect—to achieve quick results without setbacks. This pressure can lead to disappointment and discouragement when things don't go as planned. Long-term habits, however, allow for flexibility and adaptation, reducing the pressure to be perfect.

The Benefits of Flexibility:

Allows for Setbacks: When you view habits as a long-term lifestyle change, setbacks are seen as part of the process rather than failures. This mindset encourages you to keep going even when you encounter obstacles, knowing that progress is more important than perfection.
Promotes Adaptation: Life is unpredictable, and circumstances change. Long-term habits are flexible and can be adapted to fit different stages of life. This adaptability makes it easier to stick with the habit, even when challenges arise.

Example: If you're building a habit of regular exercise, there may be days when you're too busy or tired to work out. Instead of feeling guilty or giving up, a long-term mindset allows you to adapt—perhaps by doing a shorter workout or rescheduling your exercise for a different time. The focus is on maintaining the habit over the long haul, not on achieving perfect consistency.

5. Creating a Lifestyle You Enjoy

Finally, making habits a long-term lifestyle is about creating a life that you enjoy and find fulfilling. Habits shouldn't feel like chores or punishments; they should enhance your life and contribute to your happiness and well-being.

How to Build Enjoyable Habits:

Choose Habits You Enjoy: Focus on habits that bring you joy and fulfillment. For instance, if you dislike running but enjoy dancing, make dancing your primary form of exercise. When you enjoy the habit, you're more likely to stick with it long-term.
Integrate Habits Seamlessly: The best habits are those that fit seamlessly into your daily routine without feeling forced. For example, if you love reading, make it a habit to read a few pages every night before bed. This not only promotes relaxation but

also turns a hobby you enjoy into a consistent part of your life.

Example: Instead of forcing yourself to wake up at 5 AM if you're not a morning person, find a time that works for you and create a morning routine that you look forward to. This could include activities like enjoying a quiet cup of coffee, doing yoga, or listening to your favorite podcast.

Making habits a long-term lifestyle rather than a short-term fix is essential for achieving lasting change, building a strong foundation for well-being, and reducing the pressure of perfection. By focusing on sustainability, consistency, and enjoyment, you can create habits that enhance your life and contribute to your overall happiness and success. Remember, the goal is not to achieve quick results but to cultivate habits that support a fulfilling and healthy lifestyle over the long term.

Continuously Evaluating, Adjusting, and Scaling Habits as Your Goals Evolve

As you progress through different stages of life, your goals, priorities, and circumstances inevitably change. The habits that once served you well may need to be reevaluated, adjusted, or even scaled to better align with your evolving aspirations. Continuously refining your habits ensures that they remain effective and relevant, helping you stay on track toward your goals. Here's how you can evaluate, adjust, and scale your habits as your goals evolve.

1. Regularly Reflect on Your Habits and Goals

The first step in ensuring that your habits remain aligned with your goals is to regularly reflect on both. Periodic reflection allows you to assess whether your current habits are still serving your needs and contributing to your progress.

How to Reflect on Your Habits:

Set Aside Reflection Time: Schedule regular intervals (e.g., monthly or quarterly) to reflect on your habits and goals. This can be done through journaling, meditation, or simply setting aside quiet time to think.
Evaluate Effectiveness: Ask yourself if your current habits are helping you achieve your goals. Are you seeing the desired results? Are there any habits that feel outdated or no longer relevant?
Identify Misalignments: Consider if any of your habits are conflicting with your current priorities. For example, a habit of staying up late might have worked during a different phase of life, but if your new goal is to improve your health, it may need adjustment.

Example: If your goal was to get in shape and you developed a habit of working out in the evening, but you now find that your energy levels are lower at that time, reflecting on this misalignment can help you decide to move your workouts to the morning when you have more energy.

2. Adjust Habits to Fit Changing Circumstances

As your life circumstances change, whether due to a new job, family commitments, or shifts in your personal interests, it's important to adjust your habits accordingly. Habits that once worked well may need to be modified to fit your new schedule, environment, or priorities.

How to Adjust Your Habits:

Adapt to New Schedules: If your daily schedule changes, consider how you can modify your habits to fit the new routine. This might mean changing the time of day you practice certain habits or reducing the frequency to better align with your current lifestyle.

Simplify When Necessary: Sometimes, life gets busier, and you may need to simplify your habits temporarily. For example, if you're overwhelmed with work, you might reduce a 60-minute workout to 30 minutes. The key is to maintain the habit, even if it's scaled down.

Incorporate Flexibility: Build flexibility into your habits to allow for fluctuations in your schedule or energy levels. For example, create a "high-energy" and "low-energy" version of your habit, such as a longer meditation session on some days and a shorter one on others.

Example: If you've recently started a new job that requires earlier mornings, adjust your evening routine to ensure you get enough sleep. This might involve moving your bedtime up and switching from watching TV to reading a book that helps you unwind more effectively.

3. Scale Habits Gradually

As you achieve your initial goals, you may find that your habits need to be scaled up to meet new challenges or to continue your growth. Scaling habits involves increasing their intensity, frequency, or complexity in a way that aligns with your evolving goals.

How to Scale Your Habits:

Increase Gradually: Avoid making drastic changes to your habits all at once. Instead, scale them gradually to prevent burnout and ensure sustainability. For example, if you've been running 3 miles a day and want to increase your distance, add an extra half-mile each week.

Set Milestones: Break down your long-term goals into smaller milestones and scale your habits accordingly. As you reach each milestone, adjust your habits to continue progressing toward the next level.

Add New Dimensions: Consider adding new dimensions to your existing habits to scale them. For example, if you've developed a habit of daily reading, you might scale it by starting a book club to engage more deeply with the material and discuss it with others.

Example: If you've mastered the habit of budgeting and saving a set amount each month, scale this habit by exploring investment opportunities to grow your savings further. This adds a new dimension to your financial habit that aligns with your evolving goal of building wealth.

4. Track Progress and Celebrate Successes

Tracking your progress is essential for understanding how well your habits are supporting your goals. It also provides valuable feedback on whether adjustments or scaling efforts are working. Additionally, celebrating your successes reinforces the habit and keeps you motivated.

How to Track and Celebrate Progress:

Use Tracking Tools: Utilize habit-tracking apps, journals, or spreadsheets to monitor your progress. This allows you to see patterns, recognize areas for improvement, and stay accountable.

Review Regularly: Regularly review your tracked data to evaluate your progress. If you notice that certain habits are becoming inconsistent, consider whether adjustments are needed.

Celebrate Small Wins: Acknowledge and celebrate the small victories along the way. This positive reinforcement helps maintain momentum and encourages you to continue scaling and refining your habits.

Example: If you've successfully maintained a habit of writing for 30 minutes every day and have completed your first draft, celebrate this achievement. Whether it's treating yourself to something special or sharing your progress with others, recognizing your success reinforces the habit and motivates you to keep going.

5. Stay Open to Change

Finally, it's important to stay open to change. As your goals evolve, some habits may become less relevant or need to be replaced entirely. Being willing to let go of old habits and embrace new ones ensures that your lifestyle remains aligned with your current aspirations.

How to Stay Open to Change:

Be Willing to Experiment: If a habit is no longer serving you, don't be afraid to experiment with new approaches. This might involve trying out different routines, tools, or techniques until you find what works best for your current situation.

Seek Feedback: Get feedback from others who know your goals and habits. Sometimes an outside perspective can highlight areas for improvement or suggest adjustments you hadn't considered.

Embrace Growth: Recognize that change is a natural part of growth. As you achieve your goals, your needs will evolve, and your habits should evolve with them.

Example: If you've developed a habit of working late into the night but find it's affecting your health or personal life, be open to changing this habit. Experiment with time management techniques or set boundaries around your work hours to better align with your current priorities.

Continuously evaluating, adjusting, and scaling your habits is essential for staying aligned with your evolving goals. By regularly reflecting on your habits, making necessary adjustments, scaling habits gradually, tracking progress, and staying open to change, you can ensure that your habits remain effective and relevant. This dynamic approach to habit formation allows you to maintain momentum, adapt to new challenges, and ultimately achieve long-term success in both your personal and professional life.

Embracing the Habit Journey for a Lifetime: Motivational Insights

The journey of habit formation is a lifelong endeavor, one that requires patience, perseverance, and a deep commitment to personal growth. While the idea of transforming your life through small, consistent actions may seem daunting at first, it is this very process that holds the key to lasting change and fulfillment. Embracing the habit journey for a lifetime is not just about achieving specific goals; it's about cultivating a mindset and lifestyle that continuously evolves, allowing you to become the best version of yourself. Here are some motivational insights to inspire you to embrace the habit journey for the long haul.

1. Small Steps Lead to Big Changes

One of the most empowering aspects of habit formation is the realization that small, consistent steps can lead to significant, long-term changes. The journey doesn't require drastic measures or overnight transformations; it's about making incremental improvements that compound over time.

The Power of Compounding

Just as compound interest grows exponentially with time, so do your habits. Each small action you take builds on the previous one, gradually leading to substantial change. This compounding effect is why habits are so powerful—they turn modest efforts into remarkable results.

Example: Consider the habit of reading for just 10 minutes a day. At first, it might seem like a trivial amount of time.

However, over the course of a year, those 10 minutes add up to more than 60 hours of reading. That's enough time to finish several books and significantly expand your knowledge and perspective.

Motivational Insight: Remember that every small step you take is a victory. Celebrate these small wins and trust in the process. Over time, the accumulation of these efforts will lead to profound changes in your life.

2. Embrace the Journey, Not Just the Destination

It's easy to become fixated on the end goal when forming habits. Whether it's losing weight, writing a book, or mastering a new skill, we often focus so much on the outcome that we overlook the value of the journey itself. However, the true growth and fulfillment come from the process of getting there.

The Joy of the Process

When you shift your focus from the destination to the journey, you begin to appreciate the small moments of progress, the lessons learned from setbacks, and the personal growth that occurs along the way. Embracing the journey allows you to find joy in the daily rituals and routines that make up your life.

Example: If your goal is to run a marathon, the training process—those early morning runs, the gradual increase in distance, and the discipline of sticking to a schedule—becomes just as important as crossing the finish line. Each run is an opportunity to build resilience, mental toughness, and a deeper connection with yourself.

Motivational Insight: Don't just chase the end goal; immerse yourself in the process. Find satisfaction in the daily habits that bring you closer to your dreams. The journey is where the real growth happens, and it's what shapes you into the person you aspire to be.

3. Adaptability is Key to Longevity

Life is unpredictable, and circumstances will inevitably change. As you progress on your habit journey, you'll encounter obstacles, challenges, and unexpected events that may disrupt your routine. The key to maintaining your habits over a lifetime is adaptability.

Embrace Flexibility

Rigidly adhering to a routine without allowing room for adjustments can lead to burnout or frustration when things don't go as planned. Instead, approach your habits with a flexible mindset, ready to adapt them to fit your current situation. This adaptability ensures that your habits remain sustainable and relevant, even as your life evolves.

Example: If you've developed a habit of daily exercise but find that a new job or family commitments make it difficult to maintain your usual workout routine, adapt by finding shorter, more efficient workouts or incorporating physical activity into your daily tasks. The goal is to keep the habit alive, even if it looks different than before.

Motivational Insight: Life will throw curveballs, but your commitment to growth remains constant. Be willing to adjust your habits as needed, knowing that flexibility is a strength, not a weakness. This adaptability will keep you on track, no matter what life brings your way.

4. Embrace Setbacks as Part of the Journey

Setbacks are an inevitable part of any journey, and the

habit journey is no exception. Whether it's missing a day, encountering a plateau, or facing unexpected challenges, setbacks can be discouraging. However, they are also valuable learning experiences that can strengthen your resolve and deepen your commitment.

Learn and Grow from Setbacks

Instead of viewing setbacks as failures, see them as opportunities to learn more about yourself and your habits. What triggered the setback? How can you prevent it in the future? Use these experiences to refine your approach and come back stronger.

Example: If you've committed to a habit of healthy eating but find yourself slipping into old habits during a stressful period, don't dwell on the lapse. Reflect on what led to it—perhaps stress management needs to become a priority habit. Adjust your approach and get back on track, with a renewed understanding of your triggers and challenges.

Motivational Insight: Setbacks are not the end of the road; they are a natural part of the process. Embrace them with a growth mindset, knowing that each setback is an opportunity to learn, adjust, and improve. Your ability to bounce back is what will ultimately lead to lasting success.

5. The Habit Journey is a Path to Self-Discovery

At its core, the habit journey is not just about achieving goals—it's about discovering who you are and who you want to become. As you build and maintain habits, you gain insights into your values, priorities, strengths, and areas for growth. This journey of self-discovery is one of the most rewarding aspects of habit formation.

Discovering Your True Potential

Habits are a reflection of your identity and aspirations. As you develop positive habits, you start to see yourself in a new light —as someone who is disciplined, committed, and capable of growth. This shift in self-perception empowers you to continue pushing your boundaries and reaching new heights.

Example: As you cultivate a habit of daily writing, you may discover a passion for storytelling or a talent for expressing complex ideas. This realization might lead you to pursue writing more seriously, perhaps even considering it as a career path.

Motivational Insight: The habit journey is a path to discovering your true potential. Each habit you build reveals more about who you are and what you're capable of achieving. Embrace this journey with curiosity and an open heart, knowing that every step brings you closer to your fullest self.

Embracing the habit journey for a lifetime is about more than just achieving specific goals—it's about committing to continuous growth, self-discovery, and personal transformation. By focusing on small steps, enjoying the journey, staying adaptable, learning from setbacks, and recognizing the deeper purpose behind your habits, you can create a life that is not only successful but also deeply fulfilling. Remember, the habit journey is not a race but a lifelong adventure. Embrace it with passion, patience, and a commitment to becoming the best version of yourself.

CONCLUSION: THE FUTURE YOU THROUGH HABITS

Building lasting habits is the cornerstone of personal growth, success, and fulfillment. The key to effective habit formation lies in embracing small, consistent steps, focusing on the journey rather than just the destination, and staying adaptable to life's inevitable changes. Here are the key points to remember:

1. **Small Steps Lead to Big Changes**: Habits don't need to be grand gestures. Small, consistent actions, like reading for 10 minutes a day or taking short walks, compound over time and lead to significant results. The power of these incremental improvements is what makes habits so transformative.
2. **Enjoy the Journey**: Don't just fixate on the end goal. The real growth happens in the process of building and maintaining habits. Whether it's learning a new skill, improving your health, or achieving a personal milestone, the journey is where you'll find fulfillment and joy.
3. **Adaptability is Key**: Life is unpredictable, and your habits should be flexible enough to adjust to changing circumstances. Whether it's a new job, family commitments, or unexpected challenges, being adaptable ensures that your habits remain sustainable and relevant over the long term.
4. **Embrace Setbacks**: Setbacks are a natural part of the habit journey. Instead of viewing them as failures, see them as opportunities to learn and grow. Each setback is a stepping stone toward greater resilience and understanding.
5. **The Habit Journey is Self-Discovery**: Beyond achieving goals, the habit journey is about discovering

who you are and what you're capable of. Every habit you build is a step toward realizing your true potential.

Motivation to Take Immediate Action

Now is the time to take action. Your future self depends on the habits you start building today. Don't wait for the perfect moment—begin with small, manageable steps that you can integrate into your daily routine. Whether it's dedicating a few minutes each day to a new habit, adjusting an existing one, or simply reflecting on your goals, the key is to start now.

Remember, the journey of a thousand miles begins with a single step. By taking that first step today, you're not only setting the foundation for your future success but also committing to a lifelong journey of growth and self-improvement.

Ask yourself: What small action can I take today that will move me closer to my goals? Maybe it's a five-minute walk, writing a paragraph, or reaching out to a friend. Whatever it is, do it now. The momentum you build today will carry you forward, and with each step, you'll find yourself becoming more aligned with the person you aspire to be.

So, take that first step. Embrace the habit journey with enthusiasm, patience, and an open heart. Your best life is built one habit at a time—start building it today.

Habits are the small, often unnoticed actions we take each day, yet they hold immense power in shaping our future. The choices we make, the routines we follow, and the disciplines we develop form the foundation of our lives. Over time, these seemingly minor actions compound, leading to significant and lasting changes. Understanding and harnessing the transformational power of habits is key to achieving long-term success and personal growth.

1. Habits Define Who We Become

The habits we cultivate determine the person we become. Our daily actions are a reflection of our priorities, values, and goals. Whether it's the habit of exercising, reading, or managing time effectively, each habit contributes to the development of our character and capabilities. Consistently practicing positive habits helps us build the skills, knowledge, and resilience necessary to achieve our long-term aspirations.

Example: A person who develops the habit of daily learning, whether through reading or listening to podcasts, will continuously grow intellectually, gaining new insights and perspectives. Over time, this habit can lead to career advancements, creative breakthroughs, and personal fulfillment.

2. Small Habits Lead to Big Changes

One of the most powerful aspects of habits is their ability to compound over time. Small, consistent actions may seem insignificant in the short term, but they accumulate to produce significant outcomes. This compounding effect is why habits are so transformational—they turn modest efforts into remarkable results.

Example: Consider the habit of saving a small amount of money each day. While each deposit might seem trivial, over months and years, these savings grow substantially, eventually providing financial security, the ability to invest, or the means to achieve major life goals.

3. Habits Shape Our Future Through Consistency

Consistency is the key to unlocking the transformational power of habits. When we commit to a habit and practice it regularly, it becomes ingrained in our daily routine. This consistency not only makes the habit easier to maintain but also ensures that we are continuously moving toward our goals. The future we desire is built one day at a time, through the consistent application of positive habits.

Example: An athlete who consistently trains every day, regardless of weather, mood, or obstacles, is far more likely to achieve excellence than someone who trains sporadically. The daily discipline of training transforms their physical abilities, mental toughness, and competitive edge.

4. Habits Provide a Framework for Growth

Habits create a framework within which we can grow and evolve. They provide structure to our days, allowing us to focus our energy on what truly matters. By establishing strong habits, we can automate parts of our lives, freeing up mental and emotional resources to tackle more complex challenges and pursue greater ambitions.

Example: A writer who develops the habit of writing for an hour each morning creates a framework for creativity and productivity. This habit ensures that writing becomes a regular part of their life, leading to the completion of projects, the development of their craft, and the achievement of their writing goals.

The transformational power of habits lies in their ability to shape our future, one small step at a time. By understanding the profound impact that daily actions can have on our long-term goals, we can harness habits to create the life we envision. Consistency, patience, and a commitment to continuous improvement are the keys to unlocking this potential. As we build and maintain positive habits, we lay the foundation for a future filled with growth, achievement, and fulfillment.

Embarking on the journey of habit formation is one of the

most empowering steps you can take toward lasting change. The Habit Blueprint you've started building is your roadmap to achieving your goals and becoming the person you aspire to be. However, like any blueprint, it requires continuous refinement and adaptation as you grow and your circumstances evolve. Here's some parting advice on how to keep building and refining your Habit Blueprint for enduring success.

1. Stay Committed to the Process

The most important aspect of habit formation is commitment. Lasting change doesn't happen overnight—it's the result of sustained effort over time. Even when progress seems slow or setbacks occur, it's crucial to remain committed to your habits. Consistency is what transforms actions into ingrained habits, and ingrained habits into lasting change.

Advice: Embrace the mindset that this journey is a marathon, not a sprint. Celebrate small victories along the way, and remind yourself that each day you stick with your habits, you're one step closer to your goals.

2. Regularly Evaluate and Adjust Your Habits

Your goals, priorities, and life circumstances will inevitably change over time. As they do, it's essential to regularly evaluate and adjust your habits to ensure they remain aligned with your evolving needs. This process of continuous reflection and adjustment keeps your Habit Blueprint relevant and effective.

Advice: Set aside time every few months to review your habits. Ask yourself if they are still serving your goals or if they need to be adjusted. Don't be afraid to tweak or replace habits that no longer fit your life—flexibility is key to long-term success.

3. Scale Your Habits Gradually

As you progress, you'll likely want to take your habits to the next level. Scaling your habits—whether by increasing their intensity, frequency, or complexity—should be done gradually to ensure sustainability. This approach prevents burnout and helps you maintain consistency as you continue to grow.

Advice: When you're ready to scale a habit, do so in small increments. For example, if you've been walking 20 minutes a day and want to start running, begin by adding short running intervals to your walk. Gradual scaling allows your body and mind to adjust, making it more likely that the new, scaled habit will stick.

4. Embrace Setbacks as Learning Opportunities

Setbacks are an inevitable part of the habit-building process. Rather than viewing them as failures, see them as valuable learning opportunities. Each setback provides insight into your triggers, challenges, and areas where you may need additional support or a different approach.

Advice: When you experience a setback, take the time to reflect on what led to it. Use this insight to adjust your strategy and reinforce your commitment to your habit. Remember, resilience in the face of setbacks is what ultimately leads to lasting change.

5. Keep Your Vision in Focus

Finally, always keep your long-term vision in focus. Your Habit Blueprint is a tool to help you reach your broader goals and aspirations. By maintaining a clear picture of what you want to achieve and why it matters, you can stay motivated and inspired, even when the going gets tough.

Advice: Regularly revisit your goals and remind yourself of your "why." Whether it's personal growth, professional success, or improved well-being, keeping your vision front and center will help you stay on track and committed to your habits. Building and refining your Habit Blueprint is a lifelong journey, one that will lead to continuous growth and self-improvement. Stay committed to the process, regularly evaluate and adjust your habits, scale them gradually, and embrace setbacks as learning opportunities. By keeping your long-term vision in focus and remaining flexible, you'll create a powerful framework for lasting change. Your habits are the building blocks of your future—nurture them with care, and they will guide you toward the life you desire.

APPENDIX:

Habit Tracking Template

Purpose: The habit tracking template helps you monitor your daily progress, stay accountable, and visually see your consistency over time.

1. Daily Habit Tracker

Date	Habit 1	Habit 2	Habit 3	Habit 4	Habit 5	Notes/Reflection
January 1	✓	✓	✗	✓	✓	Struggled with Habit 3 due to a busy day.
January 2	✓	✓	✓	✓	✓	Good progress overall.
January 3	✓	✓	✓	✗	✓	Need to adjust Habit 4 timing.

Columns:

Date: The day you're tracking.
Habit 1-5: List each habit you're tracking. Check off (✓) or mark (✗) each habit you complete or miss.
Notes/Reflection: Space to jot down thoughts, challenges, or successes for the day.

2. Weekly Habit Review

Week Starting	Habit 1	Habit 2	Habit 3	Habit 4	Habit 5	Overall Reflection	Adjustments for Next Week

January 1	5/7	6/7	4/7	6/7	7/7	Consistent with most habits, but struggled with Habit 3.	Plan to do Habit 3 earlier in the day.
January 8	6/7	7/7	5/7	6/7	7/7	Improved Habit 3, still needs focus.	Consider adjusting Habit 4 frequency.

Columns:

Week Starting: The start date of the week.
Habit 1-5: Number of days you successfully completed each habit.
Overall Reflection: Summarize how the week went.
Adjustments for Next Week: Identify any changes needed to improve consistency.

Habit Blueprint Planning Template

Purpose: The habit blueprint planning template helps you map out your habits in alignment with your goals, ensuring that each habit is purposeful and achievable.

1. Habit Blueprint Overview

Goal	Supporting Habit	Cue/Trigger	Routine/Action	Reward	Frequency	Start Date	Progress Check Date

Improve physical fitness	Morning workout	Waking up	30-minute exercise	Energy boost	Daily	Jan 1	Jan 15
Increase productivity	Daily planning	Morning coffee	Write 3 priorities	Clear direction	Daily	Jan 1	January 15
Enhance mindfulness	Evening meditation	After dinner	10-minute meditation	Relaxation	Daily	Jan 1	January 15

Columns:

Goal: The broader objective the habit supports.
Supporting Habit: The specific habit you're building to achieve the goal.
Cue/Trigger: The event or action that will remind you to perform the habit.
Routine/Action: The behavior you want to establish.
Reward: The positive reinforcement you'll experience after completing the habit.
Frequency: How often you'll perform the habit (daily, weekly, etc.).
Start Date: The date you plan to start the habit.
Progress Check Date: A future date to review your progress and make adjustments.

2. Monthly Habit Blueprint Review

Month	Goal	Habit	Progress	Challenges Faced	Adjustments Needed	Successes Achieved
January	Physical Fitness	Morning Workout	Good	Struggled on weekends	Set weekend alarms	Increased energy levels
February	Productivity	Daily Planning	Excellent	None	Maintain routine	Clearer daily focus

Columns:

Month: The month under review.
Goal: The goal associated with the habit.
Habit: The habit being reviewed.
Progress: A brief note on how well the habit was maintained.
Challenges Faced: Any obstacles encountered during the

month.
Adjustments Needed: Plans for improving or tweaking the habit.
Successes Achieved: Positive outcomes resulting from maintaining the habit.

These templates provide a structured way to plan, track, and review your habits. By using them regularly, you can stay aligned with your goals, make necessary adjustments, and ensure that your habits evolve with you over time. This approach helps build a strong foundation for lasting change and continued personal growth.

Recommended Books, Tools, and Resources for Further Reading

Books on Habits and Personal Development

1. "Atomic Habits" by James Clear

Overview: This book is a comprehensive guide to building good habits and breaking bad ones. James Clear explores the science of habit formation and offers practical strategies for implementing small changes that lead to big results.

Key Takeaway: Focus on making 1% improvements and use the power of compounding to achieve significant long-term success.

2. "The Power of Habit" by Charles Duhigg

Overview: Charles Duhigg delves into the neuroscience of habits, explaining how habits are formed and how they can be changed. The book covers personal habits, organizational habits, and social habits.

Key Takeaway: Understanding the habit loop (cue, routine, reward) is crucial for changing existing habits and creating new ones.

3. "Mindset: The New Psychology of Success" by Carol S. Dweck

Overview: Carol Dweck explores the concept of "fixed" vs. "growth" mindsets and how adopting a growth mindset can lead to success in various areas of life, including habit formation.

Key Takeaway: Embracing a growth mindset allows you to view challenges as opportunities to learn and grow, which is essential for developing lasting habits.

4. "Deep Work" by Cal Newport

Overview: This book focuses on the importance of deep, focused work in a world full of distractions. Cal Newport offers strategies for minimizing distractions and maximizing productivity through disciplined habits.

Key Takeaway: Cultivating the habit of deep work is essential for achieving high levels of productivity and creative output.

5. "The 7 Habits of Highly Effective People" by Stephen R. Covey

Overview: A classic in personal development, this book outlines seven key habits that lead to personal and professional effectiveness. Covey emphasizes the importance of aligning habits with principles and values.

Key Takeaway: Effective habits are built on a foundation of strong character and alignment with long-term goals.

6. "The Miracle Morning" by Hal Elrod

Overview: Hal Elrod introduces a morning routine designed to transform your life by focusing on six key practices: Silence, Affirmations, Visualization, Exercise, Reading, and Scribing (journaling).

Key Takeaway: Starting your day with a purposeful routine can set a positive tone and lead to significant personal growth.

Habit-Tracking Tools

1. **Habitica**

Overview: Habitica turns habit tracking into a role-playing game, where you earn rewards and level up by completing your daily habits and goals. It's a fun and interactive way to stay motivated.

Platforms: Available on iOS, Android, and web.

2. **Streaks**

Overview: Streaks is a simple, visually appealing app that helps you build good habits by tracking your progress. It encourages consistency by showing you how many days in a row you've maintained your habits.

Platforms: Available on iOS.

3. **HabitBull**

Overview: HabitBull is a versatile habit tracker that allows you to set goals, track progress, and view detailed analytics. It also offers motivational quotes and reminders to keep you on track.

Platforms: Available on iOS and Android.

4. **Trello**

Overview: While Trello is primarily a project management tool, it can be customized to track habits and goals. You can create boards, lists, and cards to organize your habit-building efforts and track progress visually.

Platforms: Available on iOS, Android, and web.

5. **Bullet Journal**

Overview: The Bullet Journal (or BuJo) method is a flexible analog system for organizing your life, including tracking habits. It involves using a physical notebook to record tasks, events, and notes in a structured way.

Platforms: Analog (notebook and pen).

Online Courses and Resources

1. **James Clear's Website (jamesclear.com)**

Overview: James Clear's website offers a wealth of articles, newsletters, and resources on habit formation, productivity, and personal development. His "3-2-1" weekly newsletter is

particularly popular for delivering concise, actionable insights.
Features: Articles, newsletters, and free resources on habits.

2. **Coursera: "The Science of Well-Being" by Yale University**

Overview: This popular course, taught by Professor Laurie Santos, explores the science of happiness and well-being, including how habits play a role in creating a fulfilling life.
Key Takeaway: Learn practical strategies to increase happiness and well-being through habit formation and mindset shifts.
Platform: Coursera (available online).

3. **Udemy: "Master Your Goals - The Psychology of Goal Setting & Achievement"**

Overview: This course focuses on goal setting and habit formation, combining psychology with practical tips to help you achieve your goals.
Key Takeaway: Understand the psychological principles behind effective goal setting and habit formation.
Platform: Udemy (available online).

4. **TED Talks: "Try Something New for 30 Days" by Matt Cutts**

Overview: In this short TED Talk, Matt Cutts discusses the power of trying new habits for 30 days as a way to introduce positive changes in your life.
Key Takeaway: Small, short-term challenges can lead to lasting habits.
Platform: TED.com (available online).

5. **Zen Habits Blog by Leo Babauta**

Overview: Zen Habits is a blog that offers insights on simplifying life, building habits, and finding mindfulness. Leo Babauta shares practical advice on habit formation, minimalism, and living with purpose.
Features: Articles and guides on habits, mindfulness, and simplicity.

FINAL THOUGHTS

These books, tools, and resources provide a solid foundation for anyone looking to build and sustain meaningful habits. Whether you're just starting your habit journey or looking to refine and scale your existing habits, these materials will offer valuable insights and practical strategies to help you achieve lasting change.

I hope you found this book both enlightening and motivational. If you feel this book has helped you, please consider leaving a genuine review on Amazon to help others enhance their lives.

Printed in Great Britain
by Amazon